HOW DID THEY I

HOW DID THEY MANAGE?

LEADERSHIP SECRETS OF HISTORY

by

Daniel Diehl and Mark P Donnelly

First published in 2002 by
Spiro Press
Robert Hyde House
48 Bryanston Square
London W1H 2EA
Telephone: +44 (0)20 7479 2000

ISBN 1 90429 807 9

British Library Cataloguing-in-Publication Data.
A catalogue record for this book is available from the British Library.

Spiro Press USA
3 Front Street, Suite 331
PO Box 338
Rollinsford NH 03869
USA

Designed and typeset by: Wyvern 21 Ltd, Bristol
Printed in Great Britain by: JW Arrowsmith Ltd, Bristol
Cover image by: Artchive.com
Cover design by: 9 Muses

This book is dedicated to our parents,
who always managed in spite of the odds.

ACKNOWLEDGEMENTS

Sir Isaac Newton once said: 'If I have seen farther than others it is because I stand on the shoulders of giants'. This was never truer than in the compilation of this book. Our greatest debt is, obviously, to those whose words of wisdom are included in these pages. But beyond these are dozens of individuals, companies and publishing houses who have helped us along the way. These include: the staff of the York Minster Library, Debbie Foster and Ed Lehew at HJ Heinz World Headquarters, The Roycrofters Society, Allison Kyle Leopold, Father Lionel Fanthorpe, Oxford University Press, McGraw-Hill, Weidenfeld & Nicolson, HarperCollins, Random House, Houghton Mifflin & Co, Coward-McCann Inc, The Avalon Project at Yale Law School, David Hochberg, Lillian Vernon and the Lillian Vernon Corporation and finally Kevin Bullimore of the British Library who once again helped us ferret out obscure information. A special thanks to our publishers, Susannah Lear and Carl Upsall, at Spiro Press. To all of these, and others too numerous to mention, our heartfelt thanks.

'A prudent man always follows in the footsteps of great men and imitates those who have been outstanding' – Niccolo Machiavelli, from *The Prince*

CONTENTS

Many centuries ago Sun Tzu accurately recorded the
gentlemanly art of war as it existed in his own
world. Subsequently, this record has become the
world's most widely read book on how to size up,
and deal with, the opposition. We offer
carefully selected extracts from the book.

Personally a very private man, Machiavelli's classic
16th-century book on leadership and service, *The
Prince*, is a timeless study on motivating people,
dealing with 'the boss' and the competition, and
improving the individual's ability to control
themselves and the masses.

Contrary to popular belief, most pirate ships were
governed by strict codes of conduct that set out the
responsibilities of both men and officers. We offer
three of the finest surviving examples of these rare
documents.

CONTENTS

considered himself a philosopher, he was an acute observer of human nature. Two of his characters, Polonius (from *Hamlet*) and Shylock (from *The Merchant of Venice*) had vastly different approaches to offering business advice; both are worthy of study, as much for why they did not work as for why they did.

CONTENTS BY TOPIC

INTRODUCTION

The concept of 'management techniques' first began some time in the late 1970s, just before the 'greed is good', leveraged buy-out, 'every-man-for-himself' 1980s kicked into gear. At least that is what most management gurus would have us believe. The fact is that a select group of people have been managing other, larger groups of people since long before humans built their first city or ploughed their first field. If there hadn't been strong leaders the cities would never have been built and the fields would never have been ploughed. Thankfully, the words of many of these individuals have come down to us through their diaries, letters, legal codes and published works. It is from these that the contents of this book have been drawn.

It is probably fair to say that over the 8,000 years of human civilization every conceivable management technique has been tried, probably more than once. Anything that might appear to motivate people has undoubtedly been put forward as the best way to do so – bribes, holding children captive, passing out gold and titles of nobility, expunging criminal records and, of course, offering a boost up the corporate ladder, however that may be defined at any given moment. Some of these ideas were good, at least for their time; a lot more were disastrous. Some of them worked – even some of the questionable ones – and some did not. Our point is to illustrate that there is no such thing as a 'new' or 'modern' management technique; neither the modern world, nor any one individual, has a monopoly on wisdom. Consequently, the logical place to look for the broadest possible variety of tried and true managerial styles is in the dusty pages of history.

This book contains managerial acumen as expounded by the famous, the not so famous and the downright infamous over the course of the last 4,000 years. Where necessary, the original text has been modernized to make it more accessible to our readers, but we have taken every possible care not to change the flavour, meaning or intent of the original author. For the majority of entries, we have also offered some modern-day commentary and analysis. Each entry is accompanied by a brief biography of the individual concerned and the circumstances under which they came to set down their laws, codes or thoughts. To distinguish between our modern-day commentary, analysis and headings and original text, all original text appears in a classic 'serif' type while our text appears in plain 'sans serif'.

By comparing how men and women in the past dealt with their own circumstances (sometimes making their life better and sometimes leading to disastrous ends) you should be able to deal more effectively with the sages and barbarians, warriors and conspirators, courtiers and power brokers that pass through your own life.

We thought long and hard about how to arrange the table of contents. Should our 'contributors' simply be listed in alphabetical order, or possibly in strict historical order, or maybe in some other way? We finally divided them by the individuals' various philosophical styles. . . which is a fancy way of saying the chapters are grouped according to job description. Obviously, a medieval king is going to have a different approach to management than, say, a Buddhist monk. In the end, we divided everyone into the following section categories: Dictators, Despots and Rogue Thinkers; Holymen and Higher Powers; Industrialists and Merchant Princes; Kings, Queens and Conquerors and, lastly, Philosophers and Sages. These diverse and open-ended categories seemed, to us, to pretty well cover the gamut of those who have come to influence how one individual deals with their fellows.

Within these five, broad categories, the individual chapters have been listed in chronological order. This will allow you, the reader, to see how management styles have changed and evolved over the centuries and select the ones that are best for you. Are you more comfortable with the management style of a hard-bitten warrior like England's King Edward I or a Victorian-era hippy like Elbert Hubbard?

Original text within each chapter has then been arranged according to topics such as Dealing with Business Associates, Becoming an Effective Manager and the Effective Use of Manpower. A complete listing of these topics can be found in the 'Contents by Topic', p.xv.

By breaking the chapters into broad section categories and dividing their content according to topic, we allow our readers to pick and choose how to approach the book. Do not feel constrained to read it through from beginning to end. Read it in any order that suits your mood, or your needs.

It will be obvious to the reader that there are not a great number of women among our list of master managers. The reason for this is simple – no matter how competent a woman may have been, it has only been over the past century that they could even fight their way into positions of authority. Fortunately, we have found a few exceptional women who, despite massive opposition, public ridicule and sometimes worse, were brave enough to leave their mark and pass some of their ideas and experiences down to us. But even here there are hints of sexism. In the section by efficiency and manpower expert Lillian Gilbreth, for example, Gilbreth only addresses her comments in the masculine, despite the fact that the work was written after the Second World War had brought millions of women into the workplace.

Some of the material in this book may strike you as amusing, some as extreme or appallingly brutal; some will just not be quite your style. Taken too literally, some of the advice would be downright illegal! But just as surely, you will find a lot of sound information that will serve you well in your dealings with those who work for you, those for whom you work and those with whom you must negotiate on a daily basis. Time, social mores and technology may have moved on since Hammurabi was King of Babylon and pirate corsairs plundered the Spanish Main, but the fact is that human beings, and the things that motivate them, have changed precious little. Read the secrets of the masters. Take them to heart. . . and prosper.

SECTION I

DICTATORS, DESPOTS AND ROGUE THINKERS

SUN TZU

Chinese military philosopher, c. early 4th century BC

The Art of War, written by Sun Tzu, is not only the oldest known book on military tactics, but also one of the most comprehensive, and popular, volumes ever written on the subject.

Written in China during the early years of the 'Warring States period' (475–221 BC), *The Art of War* was compiled approximately two or three generations after the death of Confucius and is roughly contemporary with the works of Socrates and Plato.

Based on the text of the book, the Chinese social and military structure of this period must have been impressively advanced.

There are references to a class of professional officers, a standing military that numbered many thousands and a social system stable enough to support them. By comparison, Rome – at the time *The Art of War* was written – was little more than a collection of mud-brick buildings. The only earlier western states capable of supporting a comparable system would have been Assyria, Persia, Babylon and Egypt.

Despite the insightful wisdom of the book, there is no historical evidence to verify the existence of its author, Sun Tzu. Whoever he was, Sun Tzu was an acute observer of human conflict and an infinitely practical man.

In *The Art of War*, we find the earliest recognition that conflict is an inevitable part of civilization and, as such, should be studied as an integral part of government planning; what today we would call 'National Defence'. Sun Tzu also takes into account the side-effects of protracted social conflict such as military financing, supply, inflation, the possibility of economic collapse and the displacement of people.

More than a tactical handbook, *The Art of War* is a guide to winning conflicts in the most economical manner possible. As the author sees it, the most effective war is one that is never fought. If you can out-manoeuvre and demoralize the enemy to such an extent that they surrender without ever taking to the field of battle, you have won a far more impressive victory than one that involves bloody carnage. In short, *The Art of War* is a study in the philosophy of human conflict and the types of men who should, and should not, engage in it. The qualities that made a good general 2,400 years ago in China are the same qualities necessary to win victories in today's corporate boardroom.

The following excerpts from *The Art of War* have been edited and rearranged for clarity and consistency, using our headings.

BECOMING AN EFFECTIVE MANAGER

A good commander must be quiet, just and impartial. He must be secretive, moral and just to maintain order. His officers and men must be kept in ignorance of his plans.

> This is a hard line to walk. The most effective managers must be even handed with all their people despite personal feelings. They must never reveal their long-term plans to even the closest members of their staff who might, inadvertently, say the wrong thing at the wrong time. If knowledge of your plans gets out, you have no one to blame but yourself.

There are several fundamental factors in war, among them are moral influence, command and doctrine. The moral factor ensures that the troops are in harmony with their leaders so they will follow them through life and into death without fear.

> If your own standards are in question, you cannot expect your people to be loyal to you.

Command defines the general's qualities of wisdom, sincerity, courage and ability to discipline his men. Doctrine is organizational ability, control and the ability to assign appropriate ranks to the officers, regulate supply routes and provision the army.

> This has as much to do with recognizing, and nurturing, talent in others as it does with your own qualities of leadership. No one can be everywhere, but those who put good people in key positions won't have to worry.

Every leader has heard of these factors, and those who master them win; those who do not are defeated. War is of vital importance to the state; it is the path to survival or ruin and it is mandatory that it be thoroughly studied.

> Growth and expansion are essential to business success; but it is only those who learn how to grow safely that will survive.

A man who knows when to fight, and when not to fight, will be victorious. A victorious army wins its victories *before* the battle but an army that fights only in the hope of winning is destined to defeat. If you know your enemy and know yourself, in one hundred battles you will always be victorious. If you are ignorant of the enemy but know yourself, your chances of winning or losing the battle are equal. If you are ignorant of both yourself and of your enemy, every battle is at great risk.

> Always plan ahead. If you are going head-to-head with other companies, or with others in your own company, all the cleverness and self-confidence in the world will not serve you half as well as an objective appraisal of your own strengths and weaknesses, as well as those of your opponent.

MANAGING A SUBSIDIARY COMPANY

When enemy chariots are captured, replace his flags and banners with your own and mingle the captured chariots among your own and take them into the field.

Treat captives well and care for them.

By these methods you can win the battle and become stronger.

> When you take over a company, either by friendly or unfriendly means, integrate them into your company as quickly as possible. By making them an integral part of your larger team they are less likely to turn on you or to become a take-over target for a rival company.

SELECTING YOUR MIDDLE MANAGEMENT TEAM

Generals are the guardians of the state. If they provide effective protection, the state will be strong; if they are defective, the state will be weakened.

These are the five qualities that are dangerous in the character of a general:

A reckless leader may be killed.

A cowardly commander may be captured.

If he is quick-tempered, or rash, he can be made a fool of.

If his sense of honour is too brittle, he can be dishonoured by lies and rumours.

If he is too compassionate, he can be easily harassed.

There are three ways in which an army can bring disaster on its nation: when the general orders an army to advance when it should retreat, or to retreat when it should advance; when men ignorant of military tactics are allowed to take part in their planning; when generals who do not understand command assume authority. Any of these traits in a commander is a serious fault, which can lead him to death and bring his army to calamity.

> The above two extracts tell us what to look out for when selecting mem-

bers of management and negotiating teams. Select your teams carefully and be certain that every member of your team is up to the job assigned to them. Just because a person is good at one particular job does not necessarily mean they will be equally good at another, so base your decision on the specific job they are to fill. Perfectly competent people assigned to the wrong job can spell disaster for the project, for themselves and for you.

Generals who are capable and whose decisions are not interfered with by the king, will be victorious.

When you have selected your management teams and assigned them to specific areas, let them carry out their assigned tasks in peace. If you cannot trust them to do their job, you were wrong to place them in that particular position. Either reassign them to a place where you, and they, feel comfortable or get rid of them.

When a commander goes into battle without seeking personal fame and withdraws without orders, to protect his men, but without concern for his own punishment, he is a precious jewel of the state. Such a man regards his men as his own sons and they will die with him.

Even the best managers occasionally disobey orders, the question here is 'why'. If they habitually overstep their authority, or are just trying to make themselves look important, they should not be in authority. If, on the other hand, their ultimate concern is the good of the people in their charge, they are the rarest breed of person, a caring human being.

DEALING WITH THE WORKFORCE

A man whose army is united in a common goal will be victorious.

Command your men with civility and inspire them with loyalty and intense zeal and victory is certain. Keep your troops well nourished, unite their spirit, conserve their strength and do not unnecessarily fatigue them. Orders to the troops must be consistent to be effective; if orders are not consistent the troops will become disobedient.

> Always treat your rank and file people fairly. If they are happy with your management style they will be far more willing to stand behind you in difficult times.

Managing many men is no different from managing a few; it is only a matter of numbers.

> Deal with the mass of the workforce in the same way you would your personal staff; there may be more of them, but the same tactics will work just as well with a large group as with a small one.

DEALING WITH THE COMPETITION

In laying your plans, decide which leader possesses moral influence and which commander is more capable. Which army has the better-trained officers and men? Which side administers rewards and punishment in the most enlightened manner? By answering these questions you will be able to predict which side will be victorious and which will be defeated.

> Know the competition. Only by learning their strengths and weaknesses, and comparing them with your own, can you make a rational decision as to their ability to fight you or, indeed, to defeat you. When you know as much about your opponent as you do about yourself, and you weigh the strengths and weaknesses of both sides objectively, you will know which side will triumph.

The reason why an enlightened commander can triumph over their enemy is that they have advance knowledge of his situation. If you can determine the location of the enemy's forces, you can concentrate your own forces to inflict the most damage, while he must divide his. Probe your enemy to learn his strengths and weaknesses. Determine the enemy's plans to understand which strategies will be successful and which will not – thus victory can be created.

> Learn as much as you can about the strengths and weaknesses of your opponent before you test your strength against theirs. Only by knowing their strengths and weaknesses, and how they are likely to react towards you, can you be relatively certain that you will defeat them.

When the enemy's ambassador addresses you humbly, but the enemy continues preparations for war, he will advance. When the ambassador's language is deceptive but the enemy advances boldly, they will retreat quickly. When the ambassador appears apologetic, he is playing for time. When the enemy unexpectedly requests a truce, he is plotting against you. When the enemy fails to take advantage of an opportunity to advance, he and his men are fatigued. When there is a disturbance in the enemy camp during the night, his men are afraid. When the enemy's troops are disorderly, their commander has no prestige. If the enemy's officers are irritable, they are exhausted. When a commander offers his men too many rewards, he is at the end of his resources. When he punishes his men too severely or too frequently he is severely distressed.

> This is a short course in successful negotiating tactics. Always take your lead by judging the approach of the opposing side. By understanding their tactics and 'body language' you can keep one step ahead of them.

A wise commander must consider both the favourable and unfavourable factors in a battle. By taking into account the favourable factors the battle plan becomes feasible, by weighing the unfavourable factors difficulties may be resolved.

13

There is no such thing as too much information. Even discovering that your opponent is stronger than you thought they were is important. By knowing their strengths as well as their weaknesses you can determine their vulnerable points and those areas that you should avoid.

Those who are skilled in war can become invincible but cannot make the enemy vulnerable; consequently, you may know how to win, but you may not necessarily be able to do so.

Invincibility lies in defence, victory in the attack. Defend only when you lack strength, when you have abundant strength, attack.

A smart business person can learn to make their company invulnerable to attack; but no matter how much you know about your opponent, you can never guarantee that you can beat him until you actually go up against him in open competition.

When the enemy occupies the high ground do not confront him; when his back is facing a hill, do not oppose him. If he pretends to flee, do not be deceived into pursuing him.

Don't let yourself be led into a position where you cannot possibly win.

Follow every situation, every move of the enemy, from a distance but when the enemy presents you with any opportunity, take immediate advantage of it.

After you have gathered all your intelligence and marshaled your forces, wait until you see an opening that will give you an advantage before you attack.

The army that comes first to the battlefield and waits for his enemy will be fresh for the battle; those who come late and rush into the fight will be weary. Those who are skilled in battle bring the enemy to them and are not forced to go to the enemy.

It is always better to manoeuvre yourself into a position where you can make the first move. The person left to make the second move will always be one step behind.

All warfare is based on deception. Therefore, when possible, pretend you are incapable of fighting, when you are active, feign inactivity. Make your own forces seem inferior to encourage the enemy's arrogance. Offer him bait to lure him towards you then, while feigning disorder, attack him. Anger the enemy's generals to confuse his mind. Keep him under constant strain to wear him down.

Always keep your opponent confused. Never reveal your true strengths, do the unexpected and keep up the pressure.

Those skilled at dealing with the enemy can make him move by creating a situation to which he must adapt; they lure him with irresistible bait and entice him with profit. A skilled general finds victory by manipulating the situation.

March to the battle by a circuitous route and divert your enemy's attention by laying bait to attract him.

Your enemy must not know where you intend to meet him in battle; thus he must divide his forces and prepare to engage you in many places. With his forces scattered, those that you have to engage in any one place will be small in number.

Never let your opponent know your true intentions. Make him think you are doing one thing when, in fact, you are only distracting him.

Speed is the essence of war. Take advantage of an unprepared enemy; travel by unexpected routes and strike at the enemy where he least expects it. When the enemy is rested, make him move until he is weary. Go to places where he must follow, move quickly to where he does not expect you. Make the enemy weary by keeping him constantly occupied. Make him rush about by presenting him with possible advantages. Those who are skilled in war make it impossible for the enemy to unite his troops and co-ordinate his men. When the skilled warrior disperses the enemy's forces they cannot reassemble; when they are concentrated, he throws them into confusion.

> An opponent, especially one who is unprepared, can be confused and put off guard simply by being kept constantly under pressure. The combination of constant pressure and not knowing what your true intentions are can wear down the competition surprisingly quickly.

When you have won a victory, do not repeat the same tactics again. Respond to each new set of circumstances with new variations in your strategy.

> If you are constantly in adversarial situations, vary your tactics from one confrontation to the next. If you don't, even the cleverest tactics will become predictable.

Victory is the only prize of war. If victory is long delayed troop morale will become depressed and their strength will be exhausted.

Through lengthy campaigns the riches of the state will be exhausted. When an army takes to the field, prices will rise and the wealth of the people is depleted. When your strength is exhausted and your riches are spent, others will seize the advantage and move against you. There has never been a long war from which a nation has benefited.

> Extended confrontations are self-defeating. If you cannot reasonably expect to win quite quickly, avoid the conflict at all costs. There is no such thing as a 'moral victory' if you are left bankrupt in the process of obtaining it.

In war, it is preferable to take an enemy state intact rather than bring it to ruin. To capture the enemy's army; all, or in part, is better than destroying it. It is better to foil the enemy's tactics than to attack his army. Next best is to destroy his alliances. Only if these fail should you attack his army. The worst approach is to attack his cities, do so only when there are no other options.

The skilled warrior subdues the enemy without battle. Your aim is to take the enemy intact. To win one hundred victories in one hundred battles is not the sign of a great general; to conquer the enemy without fighting him even once is true greatness.

> If you destroy the competition in the process of defeating them, you may win nothing more than the mountain of debts they acquired during the long battle. Make your move swiftly and surgically, salvaging as much of the competition as possible and make them a profitable part of your own company. Better yet, manipulate them into surrendering to you without ever going to battle. If you cannot do either of these, avoid the fight entirely.

NICCOLO MACHIAVELLI

꙯

Italian lawyer and diplomat, 1469–1527

Born in Florence, Italy, in 1469, Machiavelli experienced firsthand the political turbulence of renaissance Italy. The Italian city states were wracked by in-fighting between immensely powerful families, each seeking to extend their power and influence – usually through violence. Appointed second chancellor to the Great Council of Florence, Machiavelli allied himself with the notorious warlord Cesare Borgia who was at war with the Medici family.

When the Medici swept back into power in 1512, Machiavelli was tried for conspiracy, tortured and imprisoned for two months. Now aged 43, he retired to the country and began writing his most famous work, *The Prince*, as a political primer for would-be leaders. Although he wrote numerous other pieces, including several plays, it is for *The Prince* that history will remember him.

Machiavelli is frequently criticized for promoting devious, or patently immoral, methods of wielding power. This is not true. He simply recounted a variety of methods that can be used for obtaining, and holding, power. The appropriateness of any particular technique was left to the reader. Indeed, Machiavelli frequently warns readers that unsavoury tactics are contrary to the laws of God and doomed to failure because they will incur the hatred of the people, without whose support no leader can survive. He did, however, caution that conventional morality is not always possible if the prince hopes to retain power. All of the excerpts below are from Machiavelli's *The Prince*. They have been edited and rearranged (under our topic headings) for clarity.

BECOMING AN EFFECTIVE MANAGER

In hereditary states, accustomed to their prince's family, there are far fewer difficulties in retaining one's rule than in new principalities: because it is enough to retain the institutions founded by one's ancestors and adapt this policy to changing events. If the new prince is reasonably astute he can maintain his rule unless deprived of it by force.

Hereditary princes have little reason and little need to give offence and ... if he [the prince] does not provoke hatred by some extraordinary vice. .. his subjects should be willing to follow him.

> Here is the advantage of inheriting an established business or office. The structure is already in place and, if it has been successful, new management need only follow established procedures to appear wise and successful.

In new principalities certain difficulties will arise. Men will willingly change their ruler, expecting to fare better. . . but they may find that they have only made matters worse. Should this happen, you will be opposed by anyone you have injured in occupying the principality. Always, no matter how powerful your armies, you must retain the goodwill of the inhabitants. . . and it is easier to retain a hold on people if they are not already used to freedom.

> This shows that a company used to strong management will be more willing to accept a forceful leader than one accustomed to lax leadership. Sadly, in many cases companies are bought out, or new management brought in, because the old management was incompetent. When people are used to lax behaviour and easy living, whipping them into shape will be a lot harder than simply taking control of an already disciplined workforce.

When a new state is acquired. . . you must be both fortunate and diligent to hold on to it. The best method to make the new possession secure is for the conqueror to live in the new territory in person. By being there, you can detect trouble and deal with it immediately. If you are absent, trouble is discovered only when it has grown serious, and then it is too late. Being among your new subjects also prevents the territory from being plundered by corrupt officials and the subjects are satisfied because they have direct recourse to the prince.

> Absentee management is never as effective as a manager who is close to his projects. Bottom line – no one is going to be as diligent at tending to your business as you are.

The new prince should also make himself the protector of small, neighbouring powers. . . endeavouring to weaken the strongest of these through this dependence. Never let these neighbouring powers build up too much strength or independent authority.

> This is very clever. If you have to deal with outside companies as suppliers, or as partners in major contracts, make sure they are smaller than your own company. If they are too large, they may see the worth of your company and try to acquire it; if they are smaller than you are, you can make them dependent upon you, giving you the opportunity to negotiate better terms on future joint ventures.

When a newly acquired state has been accustomed to living under their own laws there are three ways to retain power over them: first, by devastating them. . . next, by going there to live. . . thirdly, by letting them keep their own laws. . . and setting up a ruling council to keep the state friendly to you. The government cannot survive without the goodwill of the man who put them in place. A people used to freedom can be more easily ruled through its own citizens than in any other way.

> Note that Machiavelli suggests using members of the existing workforce as the core of your management team. The workers already know these people and are familiar with them.

When a state has been used to living under a prince, the people will easily adapt to a new prince because they are used to obedience. . . but the old ruler and his family must be destroyed. But the new prince. . . must change neither local laws nor the taxes if he is to retain the goodwill of the people.

> As long as the previous owner, or manager whose place you are taking, is on the premises it is to them that the workers will show allegiance – even if he or she was previously seen as 'the bad guy'. Get rid of them as soon as possible. However, keep their successful policies in place. It prevents the workers from feeling alienated and gives them a sense of security.

In former republics there will be a desire for revenge and they may oppose the new prince by invoking the name of their lost liberty. In such a case it is best to destroy the city. . . the prince who does not do so may expect to be destroyed himself.

> In companies used to excessive worker freedom, such as those that were worker owned or owned by a small group of close friends, the animosity shown towards a new owner may be so great that the most reasonable course of action is to sell off the company's assets, pocket the cash and re-establish elsewhere.

The innovator inevitably makes enemies of those who prospered under the old order. . . and only half-hearted support will come from those who will prosper under the new one. The support is lukewarm partly out of fear of the old order, who have the existing laws on their side. . . and partly because men mistrust change and the unknown. The populace is by nature fickle; it is easy to persuade them of something, but difficult to confirm them in that persuasion.

> Close cronies and intimate associates of former company owners or long-time department heads are unlikely to become friends with their previous boss's successor – dump them.

The most difficult time. . . for the new prince is when he is still consolidating his power and eliminating those who are envious of his abilities. Once he has succeeded he will begin to be venerated.

Establishing a new order is easier if the principality has previously been ruled by weak men who were more apt to plunder their subjects than to govern them well. In such cases the state will have been rife with anarchy, brigandage, factionalism and every sort of abuse. In this case, it must be made obedient to sovereign authority before good government can be installed.

> Even a mediocre boss can look like a star if he or she replaces a really bad boss. A really good boss, on the other hand, is a tough act to follow.

A private citizen may come to power by the favour of his fellow citizens. A principality is created either by the people or by the nobles, depending on who is given the opportunity. When the nobles find that the people oppose them, they may advance one of their own, making him prince in order to achieve their own ends under his cloak. The people, similarly, when they cannot tolerate the nobles, may make one of their own citizens prince so he can protect them by his authority. A man who becomes prince with the aid of the nobles will find it more difficult to maintain his position than one who does so with the help of the people. The other nobles will believe they are his equals and he will not be able to manage them as he wants. A man who has the favour of the people. . . finds that there are few around him not willing to take orders. The citizenry are more honest in their intentions than are the nobles, because the latter want to oppress people, whereas the people only want to avoid oppression.

> Being moved to a position of power from among the 'rank and file' of workers can put you in a dangerous position. People who used to be your co-workers are now subservient to you and you can no longer be friends with them. Likewise, in situations where, through an employee buyout, a person is raised to a position of great authority, they can be brought down by those who raised them, if their policies don't prove popular.

A man who is made prince by the acclaim of the people must work to retain their friendship. . . but a man who has become prince by favour of the nobles, against the will of the people, must. . . win the people over before he does anything else. In either case, a wise prince must devise ways by which his citizens are always, and in all circumstances, dependent on him and on his authority. . . then they will always be faithful to him.

> Keep the workers on your side even if it means replacing middle management. There are always ambitious people looking to get into man-

agement positions, but worker loyalty is rare and essential if a business is to succeed.

SELECTING YOUR
MIDDLE MANAGEMENT TEAM

The choosing of ministers is a matter of importance. . . and their value to the prince will depend on the wisdom he shows in selecting them. The public opinion of a ruler's intelligence is based on the quality of the men he places around him. When they are competent and loyal, he will be considered wise for recognizing their talent. When they are the opposite, it is the prince. . . who is open to criticism because he chose them.

> Upper management is, indeed, judged by those who represent them on the floor. If middle management or department managers are incompetent or needlessly harsh, the workers will hate them and blame upper management for hiring these people.

To keep good ministers, a prince must be considerate. . . pay them honours. . . enrich them. . . put them in his debt. . . and share with them both honours and responsibilities. By these acts the ministers will realize how dependent they are on the prince.

> The best way to keep a loyal staff is to show them you appreciate them, both in words and in more tangible ways.

It is important to discuss the flatterers who swarm through the court of every prince. . . and how to avoid believing their words. The best way to safeguard yourself from flattery is to let people know you are not offended by the truth. However, if everyone can speak the truth to you. . . they will lose respect for you. A shrewd prince must adopt a middle course. . . choosing wise men for his government and allowing only them the freedom to speak the truth to him, and then only in matters on which he has asked their opinion. He must question them thoroughly and listen to what they say. . . but he must make up his own mind.

> Ambitious people always try to get close to the boss. An effective boss has to be smart enough to tell which of these is going to be a valuable asset and which are just sucking-up to advance themselves.

A prince must never lack for advice, but he must take it when he wants it, not when others want him to. He must discourage everyone from offering advice unless he asks them for it. But he must constantly question his ministers. . . and listen patiently to the information on the questions he has asked. If he finds that someone has withheld the truth he must show his wrath.

Apart from his ministers, the prince should heed no one; once his mind is made up. . . he should act on his decision and adhere to it rigidly. Anyone who does not do this is ruined. If he is swayed by conflicting advice. . . he will be held in low esteem.

The value of advice, no matter how good it is or from whom it comes, depends on the shrewdness of the prince who seeks it.

> Choose your advisors carefully. Always seek their advice, listen to it, weigh it carefully and then act on your own best judgement. If you make a bad decision, don't blame it on the people who gave you the advice – remember – the final decision was yours.

DEALING WITH YOUR MIDDLE MANAGEMENT TEAM

A prince always has to live with his people. . . but he can function without the nobles since he can make and unmake them at will. There are two main considerations in regard to the nobles. . . those who become dependent must be loved and honoured. . . those who remain independent do so for two different reasons. It may be because they are timid or lacking in courage; if so you should make them useful, especially those who are capable of giving sensible advice. . . so they respect you when you are doing well and you will have nothing to fear from them in times of adversity. But when a noble deliberately remains independent. . . it is a sign that they are more concerned about themselves than about you. Against these, a prince must guard himself.

> Make the best possible use of department managers and people who serve as a buffer between you and the body of workers. Some may have good 'people skills', while others may be better at establishing policy; utilize their strong points, but beware of any middle manager who seems to be a loose cannon, they may be working against you.

Nothing brings a prince greater prestige than demonstrating his ability to govern. If someone accomplishes something exceptional, for good or evil. . . in civic life, he should be rewarded or punished in a way that sets everyone talking.

> The occasional grand gesture is sure to get you noticed and under most circumstances will increase your popularity, or at the very least the respect given you by your staff and employees.

A prince should actively show his esteem for talent. . . encourage able men and honour those who excel in their profession. He must also encourage his citizens. . . so they can go peacefully about their business. The prince should reward anyone who endeavours to increase the prosperity of his city or his state. In addition. . . at suitable times of the year, the prince should entertain the people with festivals.

> The importance of showing gratitude for a job well done is far too often overlooked. Everyone, no matter how low or how high, is gratified and

encouraged when they feel their work is appreciated. Don't do it too often, however, because then the compliments will become valueless simply because they are so commonplace.

DEALING WITH THE WORKFORCE

To pacify a rebellious people. . . a cruel, efficient administrator. . . may be entrusted with the fullest power. Once this man has done his job. . . and there is no longer need for excessive authority, which will soon become intolerable. . . a council must be installed under a respected leader. Each faction of the city must have representation on this council. Because the severities of the past have inevitably earned the prince a certain amount of hatred. . . the prince must now win over the people by convincing them that the recently inflicted cruelties were not his doing. . . but were prompted entirely by the harsh nature of the enforcer. The enforcer must then be eliminated. . . with such severity that the people are at once appeased and stupefied.

> If a real house-cleaning is in order, assign it to a stooge who can be blamed for any harsh measures and then disposed of when the job is done. This may not keep your hands completely clean, but by firing the person who carried out the dirty work you can quickly get the workers back on your side.

Splendid as it would be to have a reputation for generosity. . . if you actually earn one you will come to grief. Good, sincere generosity may pass unnoticed. . . If you want to be seen as generous you will have to be ostentatiously lavish. . . and that will cause you to squander your resources. . . and, in turn, impose excessive taxes on the people to raise money. There is nothing so self-defeating as generosity: in the act of practising it, you lose the ability to do so. . . If you cannot practise true generosity. . . you must be prepared to be called a miser. In time, the prince will be recognized as being essentially a generous man. . . he lives within his existing revenues without burdening the people. . . Thereby, he proves himself generous to those from whom he takes nothing.

> Trying to be too liberal, or trying too hard to get everyone to like you, can be as self-defeating as overspending and then imposing wage cuts. It is far better to steer a conservative course: eventually the workers will come to regard you as a good boss and a fair individual.

A prince must want to have a reputation for compassion rather than cruelty, but he must be careful that he does not make bad use of compassion. A prince must not worry if he incurs reproach for his cruelty so long as he keeps his subjects united and loyal. By making an occasional example he will prove more compassionate than those who, through too much compassion, allow disorders that lead to anarchy.

> In short, it is better to get rid of a bad policy, or a bad employee – even if it, or they, are popular – than it is to let a bad situation degenerate or make a stand that may put you in a bad light. Remember, it is your long-term success that matters, not your short-term popularity.

So the question arises, is it better to be loved than feared, or the reverse? One would like to be both. . . but because it is difficult to combine them it is better to be feared than loved. . . because men are ungrateful, fickle liars. They shun danger and are greedy for profit. . . they are only yours so long as you treat them well. When you are in danger. . . they run away. They will worry less about doing injury to one who makes himself loved than to one who makes himself feared. Fear is strengthened by a dread of punishment, which is always effective. But the prince must make himself feared in such a way that, if he is not loved, at least he is not hated. Above all, he must abstain from seizing the property of others: men sooner forget the death of their father than the loss of their inheritance.

The best way to keep yourself and your business safe is to take direct control when it is necessary. Similarly, it is just as necessary to keep a hands-off policy when things are going well; no one likes an interfering boss and they have to realize that when the boss steps in it is not because he is being nosy, it is because the situation demands direct action. If it comes to the crunch, it is better to eliminate a few jobs than to demand across the board wage cuts or loss of 'extras' like healthcare or pension. If everyone suffers equally, they will all hate you; if a few are simply eliminated in a cost-cutting move, the remainder will appreciate the fact they have retained all their benefits.

It is praiseworthy for a prince to honour his word. . . and never be duplicitous in his dealings. But princes who have achieved great things have often given their word lightly. . . tricked men with their cunning. . . and overcome those who abide by honest principles.

A ruler must not honour his word when it places him at a disadvantage or when the reasons for which he made a promise no longer exist. If all men were of good will, this precept would not be good. . . but because men are wretched creatures who will not keep their promises to you, you need not keep yours to them. You must. . . however. . . know how to cover your actions and be a talented and cunning liar.

A prince, therefore, need not have all of the good qualities. . . but he should certainly *appear* to have them. If he actually abides by all good qualities. . . it will leave him weak. . . if he only appears to have them they will serve him well. He should appear to be compassionate, faithful to his word, kind, guileless and devout. But he must know how, should the need arise, to be the opposite. He must change as circumstances dictate.

Since all of your subjects can see you, but few are in a position to know you, people will take you for what you appear to be, few will see you as you really are. Common people are only impressed by appearances and results.

> Briefly, be as good and honourable as possible but remember that the business world is full of immoral people. Sometimes it takes a thief to catch a thief. You can more easily get away with the occasional surprise attack if you have a reputation for being open and honest. If, on the other hand, you have a reputation for surprise attacks, everyone will expect it and your chances of pulling it off are slight.

The prince must avoid doing anything that will make him hated or despised. He will be despised for being fickle, frivolous, cowardly or irresolute and he should avoid these like the plague. So long as he avoids these. . . he runs no risk if he is reproached for other vices. You must demonstrate in your actions grandeur, courage, sobriety and strength. When settling disputes. . . the prince must ensure that his judgement is irrevocable. He should be so regarded that no one conspires against him.

> Keep your reputation clean. Only then can you get away with imposing moral judgements on others. No one will respect a boss who is more disreputable than the sloppy or crooked employee he fires for not doing his job properly.

The prince can guard against conspiracies. . . if he avoids being hated. . . and keeps the people satisfied. To that end, the prince should delegate to others the enactment of unpopular measures and keep in his own hands the means of winning favours. He must also restrain from inflicting grave injury on anyone in his service. When the prince has the good will of the people he need not worry about conspiracies . . . but when the people are hostile and regard him with hatred he must go in fear of everything and everyone.

> As mentioned above, when real dirty work needs to be done, try to have

it done by a stooge – hired 'efficiency experts' or management consultants are good for this. Whatever you do, don't embarrass your people. Don't berate them or humiliate them in front of their co-workers; it will embarrass them and make you look bad in front of the entire workforce. Eventually the workers will lose all respect for you.

DEALING WITH THE COMPETITION

Taking sides is always more advantageous. . . than neutrality. If you do not declare yourself. . . you will have the enmity of the victor. . . because you did not ally yourself with him and he feels you cannot be trusted. . . a situation in which the loser will take great satisfaction . . . because you did not come to his aid. Having now two enemies, you will have nowhere to seek refuge.

Sitting on the fence can lead to disaster and will surely destroy your reputation as a person of character and strong convictions.

A prince should never join in an aggressive alliance with someone more powerful than himself unless it is a matter of necessity. If you are the victors. . . you emerge as the prisoner of your stronger ally.

This tells you to avoid being put in the position of being the weaker member in a temporary partnership – always be the stronger member and do everything to make the other guy dependent on you.

CONCLUSION

If he carefully observes all the rules that I have laid out, a new prince will appear to have. . . considerable experience. This will make him as safe and secure. . . as if he had years of experience. The actions of a new prince attract more attention than those of a. . . long-established ruler. When these actions show skill and power they. . . will attract the allegiance of others.

Thus the new prince will gain double glory. . . He has founded a new state and has strengthened it with good laws, reliable allies and inspiring leadership.

THE PIRATE CODE

There are a few names from the golden age of piracy (1695–1725) that will always excite our sense of adventure. Blackbeard, Captain Kidd, Henry Morgan, Anne Bonny and, of course, the fictitious Long John Silver and Captain Hook.

We like to think of pirates as romantic rogues who lived a life of free-wheeling partying and devil-may-care defiance, even in the face of the gallows. Or perhaps as a reckless band, in the thrall of a despotic leader. The fact is that pirates were angry and usually desperately poor men often living on the edge of starvation. Most pirate raids were not for chests of gold doubloons and pieces of eight; they were raids for food, medicine and cargoes of rum leaving the West Indies. There is a well-recorded case where pirates held a local governor hostage, demanding a quantity of medicinal mercury (then used in the treatment of syphilis) in exchange for his release. A pirate who survived more than a couple of years at sea without being killed in action, twisting on the end of a rope or dying from scurvy, drink, starvation or syphilis was a rarity.

To keep these desperate, and disparate, bands of men together was a job that almost no one wanted. Pirate captains did not simply set themselves up in business or seize power at the point of a cutlass; contrary to popular belief, they were not despots or dictators. They were in fact elected by the crew and only served in that capacity as long as the booty rolled in. They were only in full control of the crew during times of engagement; that is to say, during battle. Even Bartholomew Roberts, one of the toughest pirate captains of all time, complained that pirates only elected a man captain 'in order to tyrannize over [him]'. The real power on the ship lay with the quartermaster. It was he who kept the food, drink and medicinal stores, settled ship's arguments, imposed punishment according to the ship's code and parcelled out the booty. But he too was elected, usually on the basis that he was generally accepted to be the most trustworthy man on board. Interestingly, the fictitious Long John Silver (of Robert Louis Stevenson's *Treasure Island*) had served as quartermaster to Captain Flint and it was this position that later gave him the power to round up a crew of his own.

In an attempt to maintain some kind of order, nearly every pirate crew assembled their own rules of conduct, called codes or articles. Anyone who broke the rules was subject to punishment. We have selected some typical examples of the pirate code. Considering the extreme conditions under which they were adopted, we think you will agree that they are surprisingly even handed.

In the texts of these codes we find frequent references to a 'share' of the booty. This does not necessarily mean that everything taken was heaped into a common jumble and everybody got a slice of the pie. Any saleable commodity, be it rum, tobacco, slaves or anything else taken in a raid, was kept in store and sold through a 'fence' at the nearest safe port of call. The cash takings from the raid were then portioned out with a substantial share (usually 25 or 30%) kept for the upkeep and provisioning of the ship, its weapons and the company.

What is most important here is that although the CEO and top executives all get a greater share than the crew, none of them receives a cut that is vastly out of proportion. When the boss gets too much it can breed discontent among the crew and make them think that the boss is, shall we say, a pirate. It also says something for giving your employees a hand in establishing the rules of conduct within your area of responsibility; just keep them aware of who is the quartermaster aboard your ship. Below are the complete texts of three surviving articles drawn up by pirate crews and their captains. They are grouped together under one modern-day topic heading.

MANAGEMENT AND WORKER RIGHTS AND RESPONSIBILITIES

ARTICLES OF CAPTAIN JOHN PHILLIPS

1. Every man shall obey civil command: the captain shall have one full share and a half in all prizes; the master, carpenter, boatswain and gunner shall have one share and a quarter.

> This provides enough extra portion to recognize the boss and middle management's position without making the workers grumble about being cheated.

2. If any man shall try to run away or keep any secret from the company, he shall be marooned with one bottle of gun powder, one bottle of water, one pistol and bullets.

> Marooning may not be practical in a business, but desertion and lying deserve harsh punishment.

3. If any man shall steal anything from the company. . . to the value of a piece of eight, he shall be marooned or shot.

> When a sailor was marooned, he was set alone on an island with only the supplies listed above to keep him alive. This may not be acceptable punishment for deceiving the company, but being cast adrift in the corporate world without recommendations or references is a fair equivalent.

4. If at any time we should meet another pirate ship, any of our men that shall sign their articles without the consent of our company shall suffer such punishment as the captain and company see fit.

> With job hopping an accepted part of corporate life, this could serve as an object lesson to those who place quick, personal advancement above company loyalty.

5. Any man that shall strike another whilst these articles are in force shall receive 39 lashes from a whip on his bare back.

> This and the following two articles have to do with punishment for infractions of the rules. While the punishments have changed, the need to spell out punishable offences, and the punishments that go with them, is still extremely important.

6. Any man that shall snap his arms (meaning fire his unloaded weapon so the flint causes sparks), or smoke tobacco in the hold without a cap to his pipe, or carry a candle lighted without a lantern covering it, shall suffer the same punishment as in the former article.

> Safety should always be held paramount.

7. Any man that shall not keep his weapons clean, fit for an engagement, or neglect his business, shall be cut off from his share and suffer other such punishments as the captain and the crew see fit.

> Everyone should accept responsibility for routine care of their own tools and equipment.

8. If any man shall lose a joint in time of engagement he shall have 400 pieces of eight; if a limb 800.

> Employee health insurance and compensation for injuries are essential both to common decency and keeping good employee relations.

9. If at any time you meet with a prudent woman, that man that tries to meddle with her without her consent shall suffer death.

Obviously, neither sexual harassment, nor severe punishment for practising it, are inventions of the modern world.

ARTICLES OF CAPTAIN BARTHOLOMEW ROBERTS

1. Every man has a vote in affairs of moment and has equal title to fresh provisions or strong liquors; at any time he may seize and use them at his pleasure, unless a scarcity make it necessary, for the good of all, to vote a retrenchment.

If individuals expect to share in company benefits, it is only fair that they are willing to share in responsibilities.

2. Every man to be called fairly in turn, by list, on board of prizes, because they are allowed, over and above their proper share, a set of clothes: but if they defraud the company to the value of a dollar, in plate, jewels or money, marooning shall be their punishment.

3. No person shall game at dice or cards for money.

Hardly the sort of thing you would expect to find onboard a pirate vessel, but considering that Captain Roberts was a teetotaller, it is hardly out of character. In practical application, this was designed to minimize the threat of fights over winnings and accusations of cheating. Similar limitations on certain liberties, if applied across the board to management and workers alike, are not out of order.

4. The lights and candles to be put out at eight o'clock at night. If any of the crew, after that hour, still remain inclined for drinking they were to do it on the open deck.

If employees must socialize after hours, let them do so off the premises.

5. To keep their musket, pistols and cutlass clean and fit for service.

Company equipment must be respected and well treated by those who use it.

6. No boy or woman to be allowed amongst them. If any man were found seducing any of the latter sex, and carried her to sea, disguised, he was to suffer death.

As in the case of Captain Phillips, sexual harassment was again intolerable.

7. To desert ship, or their quarters in battle, was punished with death or marooning.

No one who deserts their company in favour of a better paying job when the going is rough should expect to be taken back when the company is again doing well.

8. No striking one another on board, but every man's quarrels to be ended on shore, as sword and pistol thus: the quartermaster of the ship, when the pirates will not come to any reconciliation, accompanies them on shore with what assistance he thinks proper and turns the disputants back to back, at so many paces distant. At the word of command, they turn and fire immediately. If both miss they come to their cutlasses, and then he is declared victor who draws the first blood.

If you have a personal problem, leave it at home. There is no place in the office for rivalry or personal animosity, whether it concerns another member of the team or someone on the outside.

9. No man to talk of breaking up their way of living, till each had shared the amount of one hundred English pounds. If in order to accomplish this, any man should lose a limb, or become a cripple in

their service, he was to have 800 dollars, out of the public stock, and for lesser hurts, proportionately.

> The first sentence here is particularly applicable to start-up companies being formed by a group of individuals: if you start something, see it through. Setting up in business is seldom a short cut to money; just because the going gets rough, don't bail out on your partners. Note the discrepancy in monetary units: both English pounds and dollars are used. It may be an error on the part of the original publisher or simply an illustration of the fact that pirates were happy to steal anybody's money.

10. The captain and quartermaster to receive two shares of a prize, the master, boatswain and gunner one share and a half and other officers one and a quarter.

> The captain's share has gone up a bit compared with the first set of articles, but it is certainly still within reasonable limits.

11. The musicians to have rest on the Sabbath day, but the other six days and nights, none without special favour.

> Except in dire circumstances, avoid working your own crew beyond the limits of their productivity.

ARTICLES OF CAPTAIN GEORGE LOWTHER

1. The captain is to have two full shares, the master is to have one share and a half, the doctor, mate, gunner and boatswain one share and a quarter.

2. He that shall be found guilty of taking up any unlawful weapon on board the ship, or any prize a ship taken in battle, by us taken, so as to strike or abuse one another, in any regard, shall suffer what punishment that captain and majority of the command shall think fit.

3. He that shall be found guilty of cowardice, in the time of engagement, shall suffer what punishment the captain and majority think fit.

> Any of your middle management staff not willing to stand behind the company in times of trouble are not worthy of working for you.

4. If any gold, jewels, silver, etc be found on board any prize, to the value of a piece of eight, and the finder do not deliver it to the quartermaster in the space of 24 hours, he shall suffer what punishment the captain and majority think fit.

5. He that is found guilty of gaming, or defaulting another to the value of a shilling, shall suffer what punishment the captain and company think fit.

> The above four rules have the common theme of responsibilities and punishment for failing to carry them out. Laxity in carrying out one's responsibilities always carries a price, there is no reason why that price should not be clearly set out in writing. Note that virtually all punishments are to be agreed upon by the entire company. Although it is now considered bad business practice to embarrass an employee in front of the assembled company, or department, it would certainly take away any hint of unfair treatment.

6. He that shall have the misfortune to lose a limb, in time of engagement, shall have the sum of one hundred fifty pounds sterling, and remain with the company as long as he thinks fit.

7. Good quarters to be given when called for.

> This indicates that the men aboard a ship that has been taken in action will not automatically be killed if they are taken prisoner. Likewise, if you needlessly destroy a business competitor you cannot expect anything less if someone takes over your own business.

8. The first man who sights another ship, shall be given the best pistol, or small arm, on board her.

Little rewards for a job well done never go amiss.

SECTION II

HOLYMEN AND
HIGHER POWERS

MOSES

Hebrew prophet, leader and liberator, c.1,200 BC

Reluctantly obeying the command of God, Moses led the Hebrew people out of Egypt some time around 1,200 BC. For the next 39 years he led them through the deserts and wildernesses of the eastern Mediterranean landscape, searching for a permanent homeland. It was during this period that he received the Ten Commandments and used them as a basis to forge a cohesive political and social framework for his people. Only when the Hebrew tribes had developed a functional civilian and military society did God grant them the right to find, and inhabit, their new homeland. We have included both the Ten Commandments and selections from Moses's civil laws as examples of both greater, mission statement type rules and lesser rules governing the day-to-day behaviour of groups of people, large and small.

THE TEN COMMANDMENTS (Exodus 20: 3–17)

It may seem a little incongruous to include the admonishments of The Almighty, Creator of heaven and earth in a book on management style. As a result of His unique position in the scheme of things, God set down some pretty inflexible rules for us to follow. But the Ten Commandments are always a good life reference. They are simple, unambiguous, absolute and ultimately moral. They also break down into two convenient groups; how God (in this case 'the boss') expects to be treated and how His flock (in this case 'the employees') should deal with each other. This last is something all too often neglected in the hierarchy of business. How your people deal with each other can have a tremendous impact on their relationship with the company as a whole and their attitude to their jobs.

At the risk of paraphrasing God, we have added our own topic headings and interspersed a few thoughts on how the Commandments apply to modern business practice. The text has been abbreviated but has not been altered. The Commandments appear in their original order.

DEALING WITH SUPERIORS

1. Thou shalt have no other gods before Me.

> In the real world, as in the spiritual, divided loyalties will ultimately lead to disaster and a fall from grace.

2. Thou shalt not make unto thee any graven image, nor any likeness of any thing that is in heaven above, or that is in the earth beneath, or that is in the water under the earth.

> Probably not, as some believe, an admonition against art and photography, but a continuation of the above.

3. Thou shalt not take the name of the Lord thy God in vain; for the Lord will not hold him guiltless that taketh his name in vain.

> Good advice and far too often ignored. In our application this means don't mock, or gossip about, the boss and the company. If you do, it will catch up with you sooner or later and there will be hell to pay. . . maybe literally.

BECOMING AN EFFECTIVE MANAGER

4. Remember the sabbath day to keep it holy. Six days thou shalt labour, and do all thy work: but the seventh day is the sabbath day of the Lord thy God; in it thou shalt not do any work, thou, nor thy son nor thy daughter, thy manservant, nor thy maidservant, nor thy cattle, nor the stranger that is within thy gates.

While the literal meaning needs no explanation, it is worth noting that God expects the listener not to demand more of his family, employees or even his guests than is expected of himself; even God rested on the seventh day. Translation: don't be a slave driver.

5. Honour thy father and thy mother; that thy days may be long upon the land which the Lord thy God giveth thee.

While higher honour may be expected to family than work, for many of us today our work virtually is our family. Respect the job and the people as you would your own family, particularly those higher up who have helped you out along the way.

6. Thou shalt not kill.

This includes inflicting emotional damage on your fellow workers and competition as well as wiping out your competitors through simple greed or indifference to them as human beings.

7. Thou shalt not commit adultery.

Collaborating with a competitor can be just as real a form of betrayal as sleeping with someone else's spouse.

8. Thou shalt not steal.

From the company or from the competition; this goes for both real and intellectual property. If you want something, earn it or develop it yourself.

9. Thou shalt not bear false witness against thy neighbour.

Probably the most frequently broken commandment next to taking the Lord's name in vain. Don't blame it on someone else just to keep your own hands looking clean and, by extension, don't manufacture dirt against your competition, inside the company or out, just to get ahead. Eventually you will meet somebody who is better at the game than you are and they will destroy you.

10. Thou shalt not covet thy neighbour's house, thou shalt not covet thy neighbour's wife, nor his manservant, nor his maidservant, nor his ox, nor his ass, nor anything that is thy neighbour's.

> It is not that it is unhealthy to want things, even things that belong to the competition: it is only wrong to want something that someone else already owns and then set out to get it at their expense.

THE LAWS OF MOSES

In addition to the Commandments, the Hebrews needed a set of civil laws to cover their everyday activities. Undoubtedly Moses, or some of his advisors and chieftains, were familiar with Hammurabi's code. Much of Moses's law, as related in Chapters 21–23 of the book of Exodus, is nearly identical to the Babylonian code, so there is no need to repeat it here. Towards the end of Chapter 22 and the opening verses of Chapter 23 there are edicts unique to Moses and the Hebrews. These are generally concerned with dealings between individuals, making them especially applicable to this book.

All the verses have been extracted from the book of Exodus, Chapters 22 and 23. The order has been rearranged to group them by category under our specific, modern-day topic headings, but the text has not been altered or edited.

DEALING WITH SUPERIORS

(22:28) Thou shalt not revile the gods, nor curse the ruler of thy people.

> Don't talk about the boss behind his or her back.

(23:13) And in all these things that I have said unto you be circumspect: and make no mention of the name of other gods, neither let it be heard out of thy mouth.

Don't throw the competition's generous treatment of their employees in the boss's face. If you do, you may be invited to join them.

DEALING WITH THE WORKFORCE

(22:18) Thou shalt not suffer a witch to live.

> A 'witch' was seen as a bringer of evil and therefore a detriment to the entire community. Anyone who brings a curse on the business, be it by sabotage, fraud, industrial espionage or what have you, would fall under this category. Their offence should be dealt with not as an isolated wrong-doing; you must also take into consideration its effect on the entire organization.

(23:7) Keep thee far from false matters; and the innocent and righteous slay thou not; for I will not justify the wicked.

> Resist the temptation to take advantage of someone just because they are vulnerable. 'Because I can' is never a valid excuse for behaving like a brute.

DEALING WITH BUSINESS ASSOCIATES

(23:2–3) Thou shalt not follow a multitude to do evil; neither shalt thou speak in a cause to decline after many to wrest judgement.
Neither shalt thou countenance a poor man in this cause.

> 'Everyone does it' or 'it isn't really stealing' is no excuse for corrupt behaviour.

(23:1) Thou shalt not raise a false report: put not thine hand with the wicked to be an unrighteous witness.

> Don't create gossip. Making someone else look bad does not make you look good, it makes you look like a trouble-maker!

(22:21) Thou shalt neither vex a stranger, nor oppress him: for ye were strangers in the land of Egypt. Also thou shalt not oppress a stranger: for ye know the heart of a stranger, seeing ye were strangers in the land of Egypt.

> It is better to make friends with someone who is an unknown quantity, inside your company or with another company, than simply to assume they are your enemy.

(22:16) And if a man entice a maid that is not betrothed, and lie with her, he shall surely endow her to be his wife.

> If you worm your way into the business life of a smaller, weaker associate, be they competitor or friend, you are morally bound to do right by them.

DEALING WITH THE COMPETITION

(23:4) If thou meet thine enemy's ox or his ass going astray, thou shalt surely bring it back to him.

(22:25) If thou lend money to any of my people that is poor. . . thou shalt not be to him as an usurer, neither shalt thou lay upon him usury.

> Both of the above laws tell us not to take undue advantage of an honest competitor just because he has fallen on hard times.

(23:8) And thou shalt take no gift; for the gift bindeth the wise, and perverteth the word of the righteous.

> Accepting bribes from the competition, even if they come in the guise of 'harmless gifts', weakens your position and makes you vulnerable to outside pressure.

POPE GREGORY I

Head of the Roman Catholic Church, born c.540, pope 590–604

Sixth-century Europe was not a happy place. The Roman Empire was long gone and civilization had irreparably broken down. Bands of fearsome warriors surged back and forth across the face of Europe fighting for land and power. Based amidst the ruins of Rome itself, the Christian Church tried desperately to convert pagan hordes to Christianity before the end of the world which, it firmly believed, would take place in the year 1000.

One of the few progressive minds to come out of this dark age was that of Pope Gregory I. Elected Pope in 590, Gregory tried to rebuild the civil government of Rome while overseeing the needs of a Christian Church scattered in isolated pockets across the wasteland of Europe. Of all the missionaries he sent into the wilds of the world, the most successful was Augustine, first archbishop of England.

A portion of the English people had been Christian since the 3rd century when Britain was still a Roman protectorate. The population at large, however, remained pagan and England was too far from Rome seriously to consider establishing a Papal presence there without good reason. Some time in the early 590s, Ethelbert, King of Kent and ruler of nearly all of southern England, married a Christian and Pope Gregory took this as a sign that the time was ripe to send an official emissary to England and organize the church. In 597 Pope Gregory appointed Prior Augustine (not to be confused with St Augustine of Hippo), then the leader of a small monastery near Rome, Archbishop of England and sent him across the sea to a wild and largely unknown land.

Totally unprepared for the overwhelming scope of his task, Augustine kept up a running correspondence with the Pope, seeking his advice on matters both temporal and spiritual. How was he to deal with the beliefs of these furious pagans who dressed in animal skins? How did he deal with the Welsh, Celtic and Gaulish (French) branches of the Christian Church?

Patient and wise, Gregory advised Augustine on how he could best make inroads in an unknown, and largely hostile, environment. The advice is as applicable to many modern business situations, particularly for those coming in as part of a hostile takeover, as it was to a 6th-century monk who found himself an unwelcome visitor in a strange land. The text has been edited for clarity (and there are some omissions), but the original order of the material remains unaltered. The text appears under our headings.

BECOMING AN EFFECTIVE MANAGER

Letter sent to St Augustine by Pope Gregory on 17 June AD 601. This letter was carried from Rome to Britain by Abbot Mellitus.

We have been much concerned, since the departure of our congregation. . . because we have received no account of the success of the journey. When, therefore, Almighty God shall bring you to the most reverend Bishop Augustine, our brother, tell him what I have, upon mature deliberation on the affairs of the English, decided. The temples of the idols in that nation ought not to be destroyed; but let the idols that are in them be destroyed; let Holy water be made and sprinkled in the said temples, let altars be erected and Holy relics be placed. For if those temples are well built, it is requisite that they be converted from the worship of devils to the service of the true God. . . and the nation, seeing that their temples are not destroyed, may remove error from their hearts and knowing and adoring the true God, may more familiarly resort to the places to which they have been accustomed. And because they have been used to slaughter many oxen in the sacrifices to devils, some solemnity must be exchanged for them on this account. Let them celebrate solemnly with religious feasting, and no more offer beasts to the devil, but kill cattle to the praise of God and return thanks to the Giver of all things for their sustenance. For there is no doubt that it is impossible to erase everything at once from their obdurate minds. . . because he that endeavours to ascend to the highest places, rises by degrees or steps, not by leaps.

> Even before he is certain that Augustine has reached England, the Pope enquires after him. Despite the fact that your own people are not likely to be murdered by bands of brigands when you send them on an assignment, it is nice for them to know that you are thinking about them – but avoid seeming pushy.
>
> Secondly, the Pope knows that most people are afraid of change and do not accept it easily, particularly when it comes to the important things in life like religion or their job. Never insist that everything is changed at once. Making too many changes simultaneously will make your people feel threatened. If change is necessary, bring it in gradually and integrate it into their accustomed work habits.

Evidently, the above letter to St Augustine must have been sent off only a day or two before a letter from St Augustine reached the Pope. Only five days later, on 22 June AD 601, another letter was sent to St Augustine in answer to a series of questions he had written to the Pope.

DEALING WITH THE WORKFORCE

St Augustine's first question:

Concerning bishops, how are they to behave themselves towards the clergy? . . . or into how many portions [are] the donations given by the faithful. . . to be divided... and how [is] the bishop to act in church?

Pope Gregory answers:

Holy writ, which no doubt you are well versed in, testifies. . . it is the custom of the Apostolic See to prescribe rules to bishops newly ordained, that all elements which accrue, are to be divided into four portions. . . one for the bishop and his household, because of hospitality and entertainments; another for the clergy's wages; a third for the poor; and the fourth for the repairs of the churches.

Out of the portion above mentioned a distribution was made to each of the clergy according to everyone's needs. Care is also to be taken of their stipends, and provisions to be made for their food, and they are to be kept under ecclesiastical rules, that they may live orderly and, by the help of God, preserve their hearts and tongues and bodies from all that is unlawful. Inasmuch as all that can be spared is to be spent in pious and religious works, according to the commands of Him who is the Lord and Master of all; 'Give alms of such things as you have and behold all things are clean to you.'

> Distribution of corporate earnings is probably at the heart of more labour disputes than any other single issue. Obviously a modern business has different needs and priorities from a dark age bishopric, but the goal should be the same – fair apportionment.
>
> If the workers think the bosses are skimming off too large a share – and in many modern corporations they are – when times get tough they will be less willing to have their wages frozen or take an outright cut in pay.
>
> Rather than robbing pension funds – a far too common practice in the 1980s – corporations might be wise to make unsolicited donations to them. What is a fraction of a percent of a large corporation's annual profit compared with a large and favourable impression on the workers? If happy workers really do perform better, this could be a cheap investment.
>
> Finally, even Pope Gregory recognizes that the first priority of a company is the upkeep and expansion of the business. In the case of the

church it is good works and the maintenance of church buildings. In the case of business it is new tools and technology and upgrading worker skills. Anyone who neglects these aspects of their business for the sake of extra profit is not tending to the 'soul' of their enterprise.

DEALING WITH YOUR
MIDDLE MANAGEMENT TEAM

St Augustine's second question:

Whereas the Christian faith is one and the same, why are there different customs in different churches? And why is one custom of mass observed in the Holy Roman Church and another in the Churches of [France]?

Pope Gregory's answer:

You know, my brother, the customs of the Roman Church in which you were brought up. But it pleases me, that if you have found anything, either in the Roman or [French], or any other church that may be acceptable to Almighty God, you may carefully choose among the same and teach it in the church of the English. . . whatsoever you can gather from the several churches. For things are not to be loved for the sake of the places in which they are taught but places for the sake of the good things that are taught there. Choose therefore, from every church those things that are pious, religious and upright, and when you have, as it were, made them into one body, let the minds of the English become accustomed thereto.

> It is a wise boss that allows his management staff to implement programmes in the way that works best for them. As long as their programme is workable, you will get far more production and co-operation from

middle management if they are allowed to feel that they have some creative control over their lives and jobs.

CORPORATE THEFT AND CRIME

St Augustine's third question:

I beseech you to inform me, what punishment must be inflicted if anyone shall take anything by stealth from the church?

Pope Gregory's answer:

You may judge, my brother, by the person of the thief in what manner he is to be corrected. For there are some, who already having substance, commit theft; and there are others, who transgress. . . through want. Therefore it is requisite that some be punished through their purses, by fines and others with stripes across their back with lashes; some with more severity and some more mildly. And when the severity is more, it is to proceed from charity, not from the passion of anger; because this is done to him who is punished only that he may be delivered from hell-fire. It behoves us to maintain discipline among the faithful as good parents do with their children, whom they punish with the lash for their faults, and yet desire to make them their heirs. . . This charity is therefore to be kept in mind and it dictates the measure of the punishment, so that the mind may do nothing beyond the rule of reason. You may add that they are to restore those things that they have stolen from the church. But God forbid that the church should make profit from those earthly things that it seems to lose, or seek to gain out of such vanities.

Meting out punishment according to the motive behind the infraction may not qualify as blind justice, but in a situation where people work in close proximity and know each other, it can often be a far more effective approach to discipline. It is equally important that whatever the crime and whatever the punishment, it should never be seen as vindictive. If the offence seems personal, either wait until you have cooled down and can deal with the situation reasonably or hand the disciplinary action to someone else. Loss of control, even when justified, will inevitably have a negative effect on the rest of the workforce.

DEALING WITH BUSINESS ASSOCIATES

St Augustine's seventh question:

. . . How are we to deal with the bishops of [France] and Britain?

Pope Gregory's answer:

We give you no authority over the bishops of [France], because the Bishop of Arles is in authority there and we must not deprive him of the authority he has received. If it shall happen that you go over into the province of [France] you are to concert with the said bishop of Arles on how, if there are faults among the bishops, they may be amended. And if he be lukewarm in keeping up discipline, he is to be corrected by your zeal. Though you, of your own authority, shall not have power to judge the bishops of [France], but by persuading, soothing and showing good works for them to imitate. . . you shall reform the minds of wicked men to the pursuit of holiness. But as for all the bishops of Britain, we commit them to your care, that the unlearned may be taught, the weak strengthened by persuasion and the perverse corrected by authority.

This is sound advice on liaising with people of equal status in other companies or other branches of your own company. Never try to take authority that has not been specifically granted. If there are problems, it is a lot more effective to take control by example than by force. You will get more accomplished and your peers will be far more likely to respect you at the end of the project.

DEALING WITH SUPERIORS

At some point in the same year as the above two letters, the Pope sent a third letter to St Augustine. Apparently, reports had reached Rome that Augustine had performed a number of miracles.

I know, most loving brother, that Almighty God, by means of your affection for Him, allows you to perform great miracles. . . Therefore it is necessary that you rejoice with fear, and tremble whilst you rejoice, on account of this heavenly gift. You may rejoice that the souls of the English are, by outward miracles, drawn to inward grace. But you must fear, lest amidst the wonders that are wrought you may become puffed up in your own presumption. . . and may fall victim to inward vain-glory. We must call to mind that when the disciples returned with joy after preaching and said to their Heavenly Master: 'Lord, in thy name, even the devils are subject to us'; they were presently told: 'Do not rejoice on this account, but rather rejoice that your names are written in heaven'. For all the elect do not work miracles, and yet the names of all are written in heaven.

It remains, therefore, most dear brother, that amidst those things, which through the working of our Lord, you outwardly perform, you always judge yourself strictly. . . And whatsoever you have received, or shall receive, in relation to working miracles, that you consider it not as a gift conferred upon you, but on those for whose salvation it is your responsibility.

The key here is humility. Be proud of your accomplishments, but it will make a far greater impression on superiors if credit is only taken in the name of the company. The big boss will eventually catch on and if they are astute you will be recognized.

HILDEGARD von BINGEN

German religious figure, philosopher, musician and physician, 1098–1179

Hildegard von Bingen was a distinct historical anomaly; a cloistered nun in a time when women in the public eye were frowned upon, she liberally dispensed a combination of mystical wisdom and harsh criticism to some of the most powerful men in the world.

Having been subjected to continuous ill health and an endless series of strange visions of intense, and clairvoyant, religious ecstasy from early childhood, Hildegard's family decided early on that life in a convent offered their daughter the greatest security in the harsh world of 12th-century Europe. At the tender age of eight, she was sent to the convent of St Disibod not far from her home town of Bingen, Germany.

For more than 70 years, Hildegard cultivated her intellectual powers, using them to further the studies of music, medicine, natural history and the philosophy of her religion.

Historically, Hildegard is credited with inventing polyphonic music, popularly called harmony. In her investigations of medicine and herbalism she is credited with introducing hops into beer as a preservative. But it is her copious correspondence that concerns us here.

Her reputation as a prophetic mystic brought her to the attention of no less than four popes, three emperors and a host of archbishops,

bishops and common churchmen and women throughout Europe. They wrote to her seeking advice on how to administer their offices, how to deal with those in their charge and how to deal with political and religious enemies. Hildegard's popularity was so great that, late in life, she went on four lecture tours, an unimaginable undertaking in the early middle ages, particularly for an ageing woman in poor health.

As a mystic, Hildegard's sermons and letters were often couched in strange parables and other-worldly images. Below are brief extracts from some of her letters, edited and rearranged for clarity under our topic headings.

DEALING WITH SUPERIORS

O gentle father, I am not accustomed to speak of the various elements in the lives of men and what their future will be. For poor little untaught feminine form that I am, I can know only those things that I am taught in a true vision.

> This illustrates one of Hildegard's cleverest, and most constant, ploys. She is about to criticize this man viciously, but she starts the letter by insisting she is unworthy and ever so humble. If they reject the advice, they cannot be too angry; she has already said she doesn't know anything. If, on the other hand, her advice is accepted, she is respected all the more for her humility. Very clever, though perhaps not to modern tastes.

BECOMING AN EFFECTIVE MANAGER

Oh, what great evil and enmity this is, that a person is unwilling to live an upright life, either for God's sake or mankind's, but rather seeks honour without work and eternal rewards without abstinence.

Success always comes at a price, and that price inevitably entails hard work and sacrifice.

Free yourself from the low ways of avarice, so that you do not pile up more than you have, for avarice is always poor and needy, but does not give the joy felt by the indigent who desire no more than they already have. Scatter avarice like straw and trample it under foot, for it destroys all honourable standards, as a moth destroys clothing.

Work should be carried out for the sake of doing a good job, not just for monetary gain. If your central motivation is greed, no matter how much money you make you will never be happy.

The spears of malicious words hurled by the faithless and the slanderous are like a dangerous wind, suddenly assailing a person's heart. Although difficulties and tribulations from the elements befall him, he retains his self-restraint, because God is watching over him.

Anyone who strives to better themselves and their position is going to make enemies because lazy people resent success. Do not let the envy and gossip of other people disturb you.

Do not fear those things that torment you, but fulfil the obligation of your burden. And so gather to you those sheep who willingly run to you, and, mercifully, tolerate those who will not, until they call out to you.

As above, this tells us that despite the envy of petty people, good work will be recognized and it will gain you followers. The more good work you do, the more people will recognize it; it just takes some longer than others.

O you who row your boat in the shipwreck of this world, why have you allowed the infirmities of the great dangers of fetid iniquity to debilitate you through your self-imposed blindness? Let no one disarm himself, for the world has entered an age of injustice. Therefore, rise up and arm yourself against the savage spears of the lust of the flesh and the spittle of the devil.

Still, do not cast aside the rod of your authority, but hold it in your hand, just as a father sometimes withdraws from his son when that son has brought disgrace upon him. But when the son falters, he calls his father back, and begs him for forgiveness.

This is now your situation. For your sons will be embarrassed by the members of your community, who say to them that they refuse to tolerate a good and upright man as their superior. Thus your sons, embarrassed and humbled, will call you back, beating their breasts, and your administrative relationship with them will be a lot better than before.

> No matter how much people and circumstances conspire against you, keep working and do not lose sight of your goals. Don't lose faith in yourself just because those who work for you seem to turn their back on you. If you prove your worth, eventually people will respect you.

It is best if your sheep hear your voice. If they do not hear you, however, resign your office so that you can give a good account of the talent entrusted to you. For if you cannot serve well as a master over your brothers, then be in subject like them.

> Not everyone is cut out to be a manager or leader. If, after giving it your best, you simply cannot fulfil a management position, resign your post and return to the rank and file of workers. If is far better, and more rewarding, to be a good, productive worker than to be a bad manager.

Why do you sleep as if wearied by the obligation of looking after your sheepfold? Encircle them, therefore, and take good care of them, so that you do not, to your loss, hide their talent. For it is not profitable to cast aside the obligation by which you are bound. But if you see no eye of life among your subordinates, but see only their limping, then flee and cast your office aside.

Managing people can be an exhausting job, but as a boss, you must not only keep them in line, but also constantly look for the most talented workers. When you find talent, you must nurture it, and promote those individuals or bring them to the attention of someone who can. If you cannot do both of these effectively, resign from management.

DEALING WITH YOUR
MIDDLE MANAGEMENT TEAM

You are like a pillar without a pedestal standing in the street, and so you are splattered by all the mud. You are too indulgent, for you do not have the keen and critical eye necessary to condemn the black and wicked ways of mankind. Keep your mind from wandering about. Bear your burden faithfully in the straight paths, and keep your sheep in line to the best of your ability.

What Hildegard is saying here is that you have to pay constant attention to keeping your people in line. If you don't, and they get out of hand, their actions will inevitably reflect back on you. You are the boss and the actions of those under you are, ultimately, your responsibility.

The High Judge commands you to eradicate oppressive and impious tyrants, to cast them from your presence, so they may not stand in your company to your shame.

Similar to the item above, if you allow your management team to treat the workers badly, their actions will reflect directly on you.

Since God knows all things, He knows where pastoral care is useful, and so let no person of faith canvass for such an office. Thus, if anyone in his madness, wilfully seeks to gain ecclesiastical office, he is a rapacious wolf seeking the delights of power more than the will of God.

Don't be too impressed by flatterers and people who put on a show of how good they are; they are probably just trying to advance themselves. If an individual has the talent for a particular job, their past actions should have made you well aware of their capabilities.

When individuals seek after empty honour rather than humility, because they believe that one is preferable to the other, it is necessary that they be assigned to their proper place. Let the sick sheep be cast out of the fold, lest it infect the entire flock.

It is essential that you know the difference between people who are really talented and those who constantly tell you how good they are. Watch out for the latter, they are probably both dangerous and incompetent, get rid of them.

You frequently say to yourself: 'If I attempted to discipline my subordinates with fearsome words, they would consider me merely a pest, because I am not strong enough to control them. Oh, how I wish I could have their friendship without having to say anything!' But it does no good to talk and act this way. What should you do then? First of all you should not terrorize them with awesome words stemming from your office. . . nor should you use dangerous words like a club to browbeat them. Rather, temper words of justice with compassion. Most certainly, then they will listen to you.

This is one of the oldest problems of management, how to be a good leader and still be friends with those you lead. The answer here is that if you treat your people justly and fairly they will respect you; and there is no better foundation for friendship than respect.

Chastise and correct those wicked traitors and furtive opportunists who have been turned into lead through their twisted sins, those who are scattered through the iniquities of the devil and who maliciously strike out at their superiors through their great wickedness.

Do not, under any circumstances, allow any of your people to undermine your authority. Anyone who tries should be dismissed immediately.

DEALING WITH THE WORKFORCE

See to it that you show proper concern for your little garden, being careful not to overwork it, lest the virility of the herbs and aromatic virtues fail, so that they become incapable of bearing seeds because they have been worn down by the plough of your toil.

> Don't overwork anyone, including yourself. Exhausted people simply cannot do good work.

Do not hinder your sheep from taking the right paths. What does this mean? Impose lighter burdens on those who cannot sustain the heavy labours of the journey. Therefore, assign this man a task that he can accomplish.

> Recognize people's individual strengths and weaknesses. Utilize their strengths and don't expect them to do jobs they are not capable of doing well. They will be happier and more productive and so will you.

Many labourers bring their cases before you, seeking the straight and narrow way. But you flap your lips with empty rhetoric, which is your very essence, and you drive them away, angry and indignant.

> Don't waste people's time with an endless stream of jabber and technobabble. Get to the point, explain yourself clearly and succinctly and then stop talking.

Because of the tedium brought on by your riches, avarice and other vain pursuits, you do not properly teach your subordinates, nor indeed do you even allow them to seek instruction from you. You ought to steep them in the precepts of the law, and thereby restrain them, lest any of them, in their frailty, do whatever he wishes. On account of you, however, they are scattered like ashes and always do whatever they wish.

You are deceiving yourselves when you say 'We have no control over any of them', because if you were to chastise your subordinates properly. . . they would not dare resist the truth.

> If you alienate your people through harsh treatment, laziness or cruelty, you have no one to blame but yourself if they refuse to obey you.

Subordinates are no longer disciplined by the fear of God, and madness sends them scaling the heights of mountains to rail at their superiors. And they are blind to see the evil of their ways, but they say: 'I am useful and therefore I should be preferred for my usefulness.' Thus they disparage everything their superiors do, because they scorn the notion that they are inferior to their betters. Such subordinates are black clouds; they scatter the seedlings of the field, saying that they are worthless. Foolish is the indigent man who envies another's fine clothes but does not wash the filth from his own ragged garments.

> Some people, by their nature, are lazy and fickle. They want a corner office and a big pay cheque but don't want to have to work for them. These people are dangerous: to themselves and those around them. They are malcontents and should be dismissed.

DEALING WITH BUSINESS ASSOCIATES

Oh, how foolish is the man who does not amend his own life, and yet delves into other people's private affairs and, with a torrent of words like rushing waters, noises abroad all the vices that he finds hidden there. Why do you not examine your own heart and reject your unabashed lasciviousness?

Beware of people who attempt to hide their own faults by constantly gossiping about the faults and shortcomings of others. These people are not your friend, they are no one's friend.

That person whom you count as a friend is exhausted in his foolish spirit, like an ignorant infant, at one moment heeding your admonition, at the next, refusing to listen. Therefore, admonish him and do not spare chastisement.

Sometimes it is your duty to criticize the actions of a friend. Don't let someone you care about do stupid things without trying to help them – that is what real friends are for. They may get angry with you, but if they are really your friend they will understand that you are only trying to help them.

DEALING WITH THE COMPETITION

Beware, lest filthy morals become a matter of bad habit, sometimes by thinking unwholesome things, sometimes by coveting them, sometimes by actually doing them, those things that do not move one to holiness but inflict the wound of licentiousness. Flee from those things, because you do not know when your end will come.

Do not adapt yourself to their filthy and unstable ways, and don't worry whether you please them or displease them in your actions, for if you do, you will appear to lower yourself in the eyes of God and men. Such an attitude is not appropriate to your office.

Both of these tell us the same thing: never lower yourself to the level of a slimy competitor. If you roll around with a pig you are bound to get muddy, and that is not the reputation you want.

SECTION III

INDUSTRIALISTS AND
MERCHANT PRINCES

HJ HEINZ

American businessman and prepared food manufacturer,
1844–1919

Born in Pittsburgh, Pennsylvania of hard-working German parents, Henry John Heinz was a natural salesman, entrepreneur and business-man. By the age of 12 he was peddling his mother's grated horseradish and other produce from the family garden. The following year he tended his own 3½ acre plot and used his profits to purchase a horse and cart to expand the reach of his fledgling business. Within a few years his line included pickled cucumbers, jams, jellies, celery sauce, sauerkraut, vinegar and tomato ketchup.

In 1875, a bumper harvest and falling crop prices sent Heinz's com-pany into bankruptcy. Although he was back in business within a year, it took Heinz a decade to pay off the debts, which he considered 'moral obligations'.

As his business grew, Heinz took an unusually enlightened attitude towards his workers in an age when atrocious factory conditions were an accepted part of doing business. He motivated both middle man-agement and workers by treating them well. His benevolence sprang from a combination of his deep Christian faith and having witnessed terrible labour riots in Pittsburgh in 1877 and 1892, undoubtedly caused by the brutal policies of grasping industrial tycoons such as Andrew Carnegie and Henry Clay Frick.

When he rebuilt his main plant in 1888 Heinz provided his workers with a restaurant, dressing rooms, indoor toilets, an emergency hospital, a roof garden and eventually an indoor swimming pool, gymnasium, meeting hall and class-rooms where he provided free classes on a wide variety of practical and cultural subjects. There were no labour disputes, and no unions, at the Heinz company until the depths of the Great Depression of the 1930s, by which time Henry J Heinz was long dead.

As his company grew, Heinz's detractors frequently accused him of being publicity hungry. True or not, he was one of the most innovative self-publicizers of his own, or any, age. Believing that people ought to be able to try new products before they bought them, Heinz was quick to give out free samples of his products and was among the first manufacturers to offer an absolute money back guarantee to anyone not satisfied with their purchase.

In 1893, HJ Heinz launched one of the world's longest running advertising campaigns when the name 'Heinz' and a bright green cucumber shape first appeared on a keystone shaped shield. This was the company's new label and it was displayed on each product, company billboard and signs everywhere, including on New York City's first electrified sign. The same year, at the World Colombian Exposition in Chicago, he introduced the 'pickle pin', a tiny, bright green cucumber with the words '57 Varieties' stamped on it. With more than 100 million pickle pins distributed over the last 11 decades, it remains one of the most widely distributed advertising tokens in history.

Henry Heinz was also among the first Americans to grasp the importance of the international marketplace. By 1900 there were Heinz salesmen in Europe, South America, Australia, the Orient and even Africa. His first foreign factory, in England, opened in 1905 but did not return a profit until the year of Heinz's death in 1919; but Heinz never lost faith in the necessity of business expansion.

In 1897 Heinz opened his Pittsburgh factory to daily tours to promote public awareness of the spotless conditions in which his products were prepared. The tours continued into the 1970s when automation finally deprived them of their romantic charm.

When Heinz died in 1919 a long-time employee said: 'He was a father to us all. He reared us into manhood and he guided us with a kind and gentle spirit'. During his life HJ Heinz had revolutionized the food industry, the eating habits of the United States and the very concept of advertising.

The extracts below are taken primarily from Heinz's personal diary and offer unique private insights into the management tactics and beliefs of an industrial giant. The text has been edited and rearranged under our topic headings.

STARTING YOUR OWN BUSINESS

The bank president and the cashier told us time would tell whether we knew what we were doing, it was the plainest talking I ever took from anyone.

> Bankers are a good source of advice for those going into business. They have seen it all before and their position demands that they take the most conservative possible view. Their comments may sound negative, but they can serve as a practical counterbalance to your own enthusiasm.

BECOMING AN EFFECTIVE MANAGER

I worked hard all day. Seems I can't do otherwise. I do everything with all my might, which is too hard on me. I cannot bear the idea to get behind and have work push me.

> A successful manager, particularly when running their own business, is almost always a 'workaholic'.

Working hard to catch up with work that accumulated during my absence. If only I could stand as much, or as many hours, of brain work in rapid succession as I could ten years ago, when I could work 17 hours per day for a week. Ten hours is enough now.

Compulsive working is a double-edged sword: it is the only way to stay on top, but it will eventually take its toll.

You must get outside away from the desk. Your health would be better, your services in the organization of the departments would be increased, you would have the opportunity to travel and get the cobwebs cleared away from your eyes. Find someone to take your place at the desk.

This is a valuable lesson, and like so many compulsive workers, it seems to have taken Heinz years to appreciate the fact. If you are exhausted you cannot possibly do your best work. 'Down time' is essential to successful and productive management.

Be careful not to overdo it at board meetings. Give your partners a chance to say something and let the majority decide.

Your board members, or other advisors, are there specifically to guide you. Listen to them, weigh their advice and, sometimes, let them make the final decision.

DEALING WITH YOUR MIDDLE MANAGEMENT TEAM

I am trying to shift responsibilities on to others as rapidly as possible, which is a job to succeed in and make it pay at the same time without working nearly as hard as if I did it myself. As soon as I get them trained, it does help, but I find it takes three or four people to do what I could do and did myself.

Delegating is difficult for a lot of managers, but it is essential in any large or expanding business. Don't be surprised, however, if it takes several people to do all the jobs you were formerly doing yourself. This may be because they are not as 'driven' as you are, but it may also be because the jobs are getting bigger and more complex all the time. After all, that is why you brought people in.

In my long years of experience, the principles of our business have always been to delegate duties to men who are appointed for that purpose.

Once you have appointed people to a specific job, oversee them conscientiously, but don't interfere with their departmental authority.

I want to keep ahead of my boys. I don't want them to do anything I could do, first.

Here, Heinz was referring to his sons (who worked for him), but the same is true of any one of your management team. Keep ahead of them, lead them, don't let them lead you.

Very busy training salesmen how to talk about vinegar. My assistant can't warm them up on the subject.

I had five hours drill with our salesmen today. Warm them up, etc. It exhausts me very much.

The above two items show that, sometimes, only the boss can get the message across and inspire the team. Remember, it is your enthusiasm, knowledge and foresight that made you the boss.

Gave supper to all our office boys and salesmen tonight at our house. We all spent a pleasant evening and all learned much and were highly amused.

The personal touch is absolutely essential in successful management. Let your people know you care about them.

Had a very unpleasant duty to perform. Discharged James Vance for having drunk (third time) to excess so that others commented. Gave him kind advice. It is a loss to us but duty demands it. Rules cannot be broken and principle sacrificed.

G Bilderbach came from Philadelphia and in a stupor after a drinking debauch. I discharged him but sent him to Garfield Hospital as humanity dictated and sent his wife home to Pittsburgh. I feel bad as he was my assistant but I never temporize when an individual takes advantage of my absence.

> The above two passages show the down side of managerial responsibility. Sometimes there will be unpleasant duties to perform. Don't give in to the temptation to pass them off onto someone else. You are the boss and accepting the nasty little jobs that go with the territory will make your subordinates respect you.

DEALING WITH THE WORKFORCE

I called all the girls together and told them we would not allow talking during business hours except such as was necessary to do their work.

> Again, sounds over-harsh today. However, the principle is sound; setting rules is necessary and as long as they are put to the workers in a fair and reasonable manner there should be no resentment.

We are fully repaid when we see our employees enjoying themselves and spending their noons and evenings in a manner profitable to themselves. I want you to understand that it is distinctly good business as well. It 'pays', it increases my output. But I don't want to put it on a dollar and cents basis.

> Heinz's modernized plant, built in 1888, was, in his own words, 'equipped with every device of mechanical or scientific character that may be used

to advantage'. Investing in efficiency, as well as the social amenities mentioned in the opening section, were unheard of in the 1880s. The above quote is taken from Heinz's answer when asked if he made a monetary return on this vast investment in employee comfort.

When we moved into the new plant there resulted a clash and jar which caused several employees to lose heart and give notice and leave. All of which was annoying to me, yet seemed very necessary in order to make a clean start and get a good grip on the business. Several had been with us so long they had worn out their usefulness, others had swelled heads. After I had discharged some others we found we had peace and ran our business at less expense, as new men worked for less money and were more anxious to please in order to make themselves more valuable. Am still weeding out some who have been with us too long.

Some employee discontent is inevitable in any working environment, especially when changes are implemented. Some of Heinz's employees left when the plant moved and others he felt he needed to dismiss for greater efficiency. It is up to the boss to make the necessary changes that will keep the company running smoothly and profitably.

Ira Kimmel left us after a week's notice. He thought he could do better. We pay him $75 per month and that more because of character and honesty than ability. He thanks me for friendship, etc. We are under the impression that he goes to a new position.

Losing a long-time employee is always stressful, but the desire of one of your people to better themselves is no reason for bitterness. After all, you probably did the same thing on your way up.

DEALING WITH THE COMPETITION

We saw a printed business card. Watkins and Kimmel, Pickles and Preserving Business. All are surprised as Ira's business ability is limited. I wish him well. There is plenty of room at the top.

> One week after Ira Kimmel (see the passage above) left the Heinz company, HJ Heinz found that he had gone into business for himself. Amazingly, Heinz seemed to harbour no animosity against his former employee. He had complete faith in his own product and knew it was a big market. There was no reason for bitterness.

Met with a Committee of Preserves Manufacturers relative to forming a trust of all the preservers in the United States this side of the Missouri River. We prefer to remain outside.

> When your own company is superior to the competition there is no need to seek protection in numbers. It might even tarnish your image to ally yourself with less reputable companies.

MANAGING A SUBSIDIARY COMPANY

In Denver. I looked up our agency here. Find all well, but they need waking up and organizing anew, which I am now at. . . Hard knocks and well directed efforts will help some here at this new agency.

> Never let a subsidiary company forget who's boss. Frequent visits and personal attention are essential to keeping things running smoothly at all of your branches.

I was very much pleased with the system and order of the old Batty factory (in England) now Heinz Number 11 Factory. We have increased output 50% since putting on the new style labels and bottles. We pack only for Continental Europe and export under the Batty label where the goods were introduced in 1824, while in Great Britain we offer no Batty foods for sale except when the trade demands some of the sauces that were formerly well known.

I was the only one who had any faith in the future development of the 57 through a branch house in England. It required hard work to continue for years at a loss to introduce the goods, but after ten years the tide turned and we are now practically running the business on the same average cost as in the United States.

> Opening up new markets and territories can be a long, hard and nerve-wracking job, particularly when you are not there to oversee the day-to-day operation of the new branch. This is not a step to be taken by the faint-hearted.

PUBLIC RELATIONS

. . .The idea of 57 varieties gripped me at once. I jumped off the train and began the work of laying out my advertising plans. Within a week the sign of the green pickle with the '57 Varieties' was appearing in newspapers, on billboards, signs and everywhere else I could find to stick it.

> On a New York City elevated railway car, Heinz saw a poster advertising '21 styles' of shoes. Although he already manufactured more than 60 varieties of condiments, he was struck by the idea of using the number 57 on the company's logo. The success of the idea proves that clever advertising gimmicks can be hugely successful.

If things are not brisk, I am willing to borrow money in order to reach people who can afford to buy. If my methods of advertising have been a failure the world at large would have made the discovery e'er this. I now insist that we act. I urged this before I left home but cannot find a single advertisement in the magazines. Are you asleep? Read this to the advertising department.

Continuing to advertise during recessions or down-turns in business is essential to keep your company in the public eye. Better times will come, but if people forget your company name you may never regain the lost revenues.

FINANCIAL DEALINGS (BANKRUPTCY)

I have been nearly killed and crazed at times meeting and protecting cheques. We fear we cannot pay notes as they come due. Yet we have had nothing go to protest court. We always pay. As we go on, we renew [our resources].

On the brink of bankruptcy, Heinz struggled hard to keep his company afloat and operating. He paid his debts and prevented himself from being sued for non-payment.

We found matters were in such shape that we could not save our business but must let it go. Oh, what a thought to give up all after working so hard for ten years, besides getting many friends and parents in trouble with us.

Bankruptcy is a traumatizing experience for anyone. The trick is not to give up, learn from the experience and keep going.

I find there are few friends when we are known to have no cash and are bankrupt. I feel very sad, as though every person had lost confidence in me and I had not a true friend in the world. A man is nowhere without money.

Feelings of isolation, both personally and in the business community, are frequent side-effects of business failure.

I resolve not to worry as much about our trouble, as it will not better it. People will censure us no matter what we do.

Christy, my lawyer, asked for $400 or $500 to use as he saw fit to quiet several people and get me out of bankruptcy. This is, and was, quite a temptation. I decided no. Honourably or not at all.

Heinz's honesty in refusing to buy his way out of trouble helped regain the respect of his peers, creditors and the newspapers which had been relentless in their criticism.

MAXIMS AND CLEVER SAYINGS

Like many people who lived during the sentimental, late Victorian era, Henry J Heinz loved clever sayings. He adorned the walls of his offices, workers' cafeterias and work areas with them. They were even worked into the stained glass windows of company assembly halls. Below are a few of the more practical.

HJ HEINZ'S 'EIGHT IMPORTANT IDEAS'

1. Housewives will pay someone else to take over a share of their more tedious kitchen work.

Heinz may have made food products, but the same principle applies in any field. If you can make someone's life easier through your service or product, you have achieved the first step towards success.

2. A pure article of superior quality, will find a ready market through its own intrinsic merit, if it is properly packaged and promoted.

Marketing is the key here. Tragically, even poor quality products and services, properly 'hyped', can rise to be market leaders, but it is unusual for them to last. The combination of a good product and creative marketing is essential to long-term success.

3. To improve the finished product that comes out of the bottle, can or crock, you must improve it in the ground where it is grown.

In Heinz's case this was the literal truth, but the same is true metaphorically. You can not produce a finished product of quality if its component parts are inferior.

4. Our market is the world.

Never limit yourself to a known territory or an established client list. Success depends on expansion and Heinz was undoubtedly one of the first men to think in global terms.

5. Harmonize the business system of today and you will have the remedy for the present discontent that characterizes the commercial world and fosters the spirit of enmity between capital and labour.

If management and labour can't get along, there will inevitably be trouble.

6. We keep our shingle out and then let the public blow our horn, and that counts. But we must do something to make them do this.

Word of mouth and peer pressure are the best publicity there is, but it is up to you to start the public talking.

7. Government regulation will help the food processing industry grow.

The point is that a competently made and safe product has nothing to fear from health and safety regulations.

8. Religion is world loyalty.

A man of devout faith, Heinz was convinced that religion was the answer to the world's problems. Agree or not, it is fair to say that people of goodwill, working together, is a fine start.

The following epigrams decorated the walls and windows of Heinz's factories and offices. As they are brief and self-explanatory, no comment seems necessary.

Quality is to a product what character is to a man.

We are working for success, not for money. The money will take care of itself.

It is neither capital nor labour that brings success, but management, because management can attract capital and capital can employ labour.

To do a common thing uncommonly well brings success.

Heart power is better than horse power.

It's not so much what you say, but how, when and where you say it.

A young man's integrity is the keystone to his success.

Make all you can honestly, save all you can prudently, give all you can wisely.

Do the best you can, where you are, with what you have today.

Find your place and fill it.

Luck may help a man over a ditch if he jumps well.

HELENA RUBINSTEIN

Polish–American businesswoman and cosmetics manufacturer,
1870–1965

Madame Helena Rubinstein was a complete anomaly in the business world. Trained in her native Poland as a physician, she began her career in the cosmetics industry in 1902 with 12 jars of facial cream concocted by her mother. Over the next half century she parlayed her knowledge of science, with an uncanny sense of public relations, into a personal fortune worth more than 50 million dollars. By the early 1950s her 52% holding in the Helena Rubinstein cosmetics firm alone was worth more than 30 million dollars.

Personally, Helena Rubinstein was extremely difficult. She was tight with money, pushy, impossible to work for and extraordinarily eccentric. She collected everything from great art to fine furniture and kept shoe boxes stuffed with money and jewels under her bed.

Working entirely on intuition, she never set down hard and fast rules on company policy, but delivered a constant stream of orders to her employees in a staccato, 'machine-gun' delivery that drove her assistants to distraction. She had an overbearing, yet almost magical way of moulding her management team to her ever-changing business plans.

Never afraid to copy and adapt other companies' work, Madame Rubinstein drove her firm along two distinct yet interconnected lines. First was what she referred to as 'the bread and butter stuff': the tried and tested lines of beauty creams and make-up that had become mainstays of the international cosmetics industry. As an adjunct to these products, she continually introduced novelty items and gimmicks that kept her product lines fresh and constantly in the public eye.

Following are selected 'gems' of Rubinstein's wisdom extracted from

Madame, the published memoirs of her long-time assistant, Patrick O'Higgins. As you will see, it was in the arena of public relations that Helena Rubinstein really shone. The extracts have been edited and rearranged for consistency within our topic headings.

BECOMING AN EFFECTIVE MANAGER

I am a merchant. To be a good merchant, you need a sharp eye. I know a good thing when I hear it and I like quick decisions. Take advantage of the situation. Every situation. That and hard work.

When you need work, take anything you can get. Then you can improve yourself.

> It is no secret that getting ahead demands hard work. Both of the above quotes show that even someone as successful as Rubinstein realized that the only way to stay ahead, once you get there, is to keep working hard. Anyone who rests on their laurels is courting disaster.

Listen. Say less than more. If you want to be smart, play stupid. Take a walk around the building. Find things out. That's how you'll learn.

> Understanding the workforce is essential to success; it allows you to spot small problems before they get out of hand, and to gauge the strengths and weaknesses of your people. When management allows itself to become isolated from the workers it will almost certainly make mistakes that could have been avoided.

I always lived over the shops until we expanded and I was forced to move into apartments. So I bought the apartments. Next I bought the buildings. Then I built the buildings. Why not? Real estate is a good thing to have.

Diversification is not only a key to success, prudently done it is a solid hedge against the uncertainties of a volatile market.

Anyone interested in money must study the stock exchange.

It probably goes without saying, but if you compete in the world of national or international business, it is essential to understand the larger trends in the world's marketplace.

DEALING WITH YOUR
MIDDLE MANAGEMENT TEAM

Keep them on their toes!

Rubinstein loved to send out sharp, terse, and often cryptic, messages and memos. An employee's ability to decipher them was one of the ways she gauged the quality of her managerial staff.

Are you learning? Are you getting stronger? It's all up to you. You must now be strong and do something really worthwhile.

After a brief introduction into the world of Rubinstein cosmetics, Madame Rubinstein often cut middle management recruits loose to find their own level in the company. How well they coped with being set adrift quickly determined their future with the company.

PUBLIC RELATIONS

Public relations, that's what you must concentrate on. There's nothing like a clever stunt to get something off the ground.

A master of promotion, when Rubinstein launched her 'Heaven Sent' fragrance she dropped hundreds of balloons on New York's Fifth Avenue, attached to each was a sample of the new product with the note: 'A gift for you from Heaven.'

First you have to have a good story to give. Next you must know how to give it. Last, call up the most important newspapers. Start at the top! After that it's all luck, contacts and people who know how to spread the gospel. . . my gospel.

> Even if she hired people to come up with these 'good stories', it was Rubinstein herself who generally delivered them. She understood the importance of the personal touch and used it to tremendous success. Many top managers who keep out of sight and allow their press office and advertising people to do their leg work might do well to emulate this approach. It is exhausting, but it works.

Public relations is just blah-blah; but to be really useful the blah-blah has to be merchandised. No use in publicizing a product unless it sells. A good free write-up is worth ten ads. . . but the secret of public relations is making friends with the press; knowing how to use them. A really clever press release is one way. It can save them a lot of work.

> Again, Rubinstein always knew how to get the most mileage for the least money – the most bang for her buck. By catering to the personal vanities of the press and trendsetters of her day, she garnered massive publicity that would have cost millions had it simply been bought through an advertising agency.

Entertaining is good for publicity.

> Most business people engage in some form of entertaining, even if it is just buying drinks for business associates. Rubinstein, however, preferred the occasional lavish dinner to the constant hassle and expense of casual get-togethers designed to reinforce business associations. Styles of entertaining may have changed dramatically since Rubinstein's day, but the underlying message remains sound.

Here, I want you to have this. Take it for luck. It brought me luck and it will bring you luck too. It is always better if you give people something that you treasure.

> Madame Rubinstein loved to give gifts of jewellery to business associates, members of the press and important clients, selecting appropriate pieces from piles of jewellery she kept expressly for this purpose. She would always wear items she was about to give away; believing that if the gift appeared to be a personal favourite, it would leave an impression worth far more than the cost of the item itself.

Customers, particularly future customers, are not to be sneezed at. Besides, a little sample won't ruin us and I've made a friend; wait and see, she'll spread the gospel.

> When approached by the public, Rubinstein always took a moment to talk to them and answer their questions on skin care; taking their names and addresses so she could send samples of appropriate products. It cost far less than expensive advertising and, she insisted, made customers for life.

Why blabber [about your successes]? It only makes people envious and it brings beggars to the door.

> Rubinstein refused publicly to address the issue of her wealth, firmly believing the image of someone struggling along bravely in the face of massive competition was a useful, and sympathetic, public image.

DEALING WITH THE COMPETITION

No sooner do we bring out something new than Revlon copies us. They are busy in there copying us. . . I swear. They're nothing but copy-cats. I call it downright dishonest.

> Although she, herself, was not above adapting another company's products, it drove her to distraction when the competition copied her ideas.

When Revlon copied her best-selling product lines it infuriated her, but she turned competition to her advantage by purchasing large blocks of stock in the Revlon Corporation.

LILLIAN VERNON

German-American businesswoman 1927–

When ten-year-old Lillian Menasche and her family landed in New York in 1937 they had lost their home, their business, all of their money and did not speak the language. They were among the lucky ones – many who could not escape Hitler's Germany would be far less fortunate.

With the support of her struggling father, Lillian eventually attended New York University, but dropped out to get married after only two years.

By 1951 Lillian and Sam Hochberg were living in a small apartment in Mount Vernon, New York. Sam's job barely covered their expenses and Lillian was pregnant. Lillian was determined to earn extra cash but at the time it was unacceptable for a pregnant woman to work out-side the home. When she told her husband she was going to set up a mail-order business he asked her what she was going to sell: 'I don't know, but I'll think of something' was her only reply.

With the help of her father, now a leather goods manufacturer, Lillian placed an ad in *Seventeen* magazine for monogrammed belt and hand-bag sets. The ad cost $495.00 and within three months had generated $32,000.00 worth of sales; overseen and managed from the family's kitchen table. Building on this unexpected success, Lillian Hochberg adopted the name Lillian Vernon (taken from the name of the town in which they lived), and began building one of America's largest sole-owned mail-order companies.

Through careful shepherding of her fledgling company, and never wasting anything, by 1963 Lillian Vernon had become a small but stable direct mail catalogue firm dealing in decorative and practical housewares. That same year they became an accessories supplier for the cosmetics giant Revlon.

Lillian Vernon insists that success can come from unexpected quarters. In her case, it was the 1973–74 oil embargo and fuel crisis. Unable to drive to their usual stores and shops, Americans turned to mail-order catalogues to supply their needs. Since then, an ever increasing number of working women have found that catalogue shopping allows them greater amounts of free time.

By the mid 1990s the Lillian Vernon Corporation was a vast $238 million dollar enterprise overseen by 14 senior managers. Now nearing 70, Lillian Vernon still kept an active role in the business, leading shopping expeditions all over the world in search of new products to offer to her customers.

Having learned to be an effective manager the hard way, Lillian Vernon has always been willing to share her knowledge with others. There follows a few of her personal observations on starting and running a business, taken from Lillian Vernon's autobiography *An Eye For Winners*. The excerpts have been edited and rearranged under our topic headings.

STARTING YOUR OWN BUSINESS

Sometimes it's easier to start a new business than keep a tired one going.

> It is perfectly natural to try to keep an existing business alive, but it is not always the most economically feasible course of action.

If you have never worked before you may be better equipped to go into business for yourself than people who have acquired an office mentality. It is common for someone accustomed to working with others to feel isolated when setting up shop on their own.

> Running your own business is unquestionably isolating and requires massive self-discipline.

Social outsiders have an advantage in the business world. Outsiders see people and the world with a special, objective clarity. You are now your own boss, working on your own turf. This will be your source of strength.

> Individuals not accustomed to being 'one of the crowd' are less likely to have problems striking out on their own.

All innovations originate with an idea – a vision. And every idea that led somewhere was supported by solid research and hard work. The successful entrepreneur learns to be a practical visionary.

> Vision is a great advantage; practicality is essential.

My warning to all entrepreneurs. When someone gives you the look that says 'You're a gambler who doesn't know when to stop'; turn away and ignore it. I wish I knew how to do that without giving offence, but I never learned. Perhaps it isn't possible.

> But do be smart enough to listen to, and consider, sound advice from experienced people.

Instinct will get you started, but it won't sustain you; after all, your competitors have instinct too. So you have to augment your natural gifts with good strategic planning and day-to-day immersion in the nitty-gritty of your enterprise. Without the proper amount of each ingredient, you won't capture the winning edge. In business, attention to detail is crucial.

No matter what business you are going into – even if you work at home – you will have start-up costs. Keep them to a minimum. . . but anticipate your expenditures and formulate an initial budget. . . Plan for increases in all your expenses.

> The more money there is available, the more likelihood of it being squandered. Even if you have plenty, run your business close to the line. It is the surest way to gauge how much you are really making.

Bootstrapping is the word we use to describe starting a business with very little money. To keep going, bootstrappers rely completely on their wits to generate a sustaining cash flow. . . You have to hold a tight budget and use every technique you can to generate cash simply to stay alive. A bootstrapper gears every outlay toward maximizing cash flow and cuts costs and corners any way possible. Beginners must never forget that the key to business success is money.

> Any smart business person does the same, otherwise they risk squandering company profit.

Despite my early successes, I still followed my basic rule of thumb; invest like a Rockefeller, live like a pauper. I run my company like a French housewife – no leftovers.

> Waste is lost money and the larger the business the greater the potential for waste. Consider how government bureaucracies operate.

You must aim for liquidity; cash. There are misunderstandings about the word cash; profits are not cash, accounts receivable are not cash until they are received and physical assets are not cash.

> Liquid assets, cash, are only that: cash. Anything else is either an asset or a debt.

The foundation of future business success is your product or service. You must offer something that people want to buy. Keep your mind open to ideas for products and services that might satisfy needs. Also watch for ways to improve what is already on the market. Right from the start I gave people what they wanted at a price they could afford. Practical considerations always guided me.

Research your market. Ask yourself whether your idea and the way you execute it is better than what's already out there. The answer must be an unequivocal *yes*, otherwise you won't be competitive. Buy and test similar products.

> Before investing your time and money it is essential that you know both your target market and the competition that is there ahead of you. If you don't understand both of these you risk disaster.

One of your earliest and most crucial decisions will concern your opening inventory. How much should you have on hand when you start? Keep inventories low: until you can project your sales, your inventory should be as tight as possible. Remember that every dollar tied up in inventory leaves a dollar less for other expenses.

Concentration is the key to economic success. Concentrate on the products you know how to sell and on the market with which you are familiar. Stay in the business you know. Develop short-term and long-term goals, but concentrate on present priorities. It is tempting for a new entrepreneur to speed ahead as quickly as possible. My advice is to research and test. Stick with one or two products and don't add more until you have established your market. Then add as quickly as possible. Above all, you will accumulate cash, which can keep your company afloat when you begin to expand.

> Realize how hard it is to 'add as quickly as possible' and simultaneously 'accumulate cash'. Both are essential to growth, but balancing one against the other requires very careful management.

Growth brings opportunities and complications. The opportunities for making money – maybe a lot of it – are there, but before that can happen you may find yourself coping with unexpected problems. . . All your expenses will take an enormous leap. . . Increasing sales also means you must invest in more product, warehousing and fulfilment. You have to hire more employees and most likely you will need larger quarters.

> At least as many businesses fail due to rapid expansion as to lack of business. It is frighteningly easy to be so successful that you go broke.

By far the simplest type of business structure is the sole proprietorship. You are alone in the business. There are no shares and therefore no division of potential profits. You call the shots. Financial liability is, however, the chief drawback to this arrangement.

> Not only financial liability, but emotional liability. You need someone to help make decisions and discuss strategy. Unless you have sound managerial experience, it may be wise to consider a partner or find the money to hire a reliable manager.

A partnership arrangement is relatively easy to set up and a partner can bring much needed cash, experience and support into the fledgling business. With a partner you have someone with whom you can discuss problems, map out strategy and formulate goals. If you find that the partnership does not work out as you hoped it would, it can be dissolved by conducting a buy-out or closing the business.

> If you are going to take on a partner, be sure they have something beyond money to offer. One of you needs to have business and managerial experience.

A corporation is a distinct legal entity with limited liability. Forming a corporation can be a complex and expensive procedure that calls for expert legal advice.

As a start-up business this is probably unnecessary unless you are in a high-risk business.

BECOMING AN EFFECTIVE MANAGER

It is always important to keep your ears open and stay alert. Sometimes an unexpected set of lucky circumstances simply falls into place.

See the previous discussion of the effect on Lillian Vernon's catalogue of the 1973–74 oil embargo.

I long ago learned that the only way to learn is to keep quiet, look and listen.

In business you just can't rest on your laurels; if you're not moving forward, you're slipping behind.

But don't forget to take time to consolidate now and again. Constant growth is economically and emotionally draining.

Resilience is an essential ingredient when running a business.

Never forget that there are limits to the human body's endurance. If you find yourself working 12 hours a day, snatching food instead of sitting down to meals and never taking time away from your company, you will hurt your business – but even more important, you will hurt yourself. You do a good job only if you are healthy and mentally alert.

Many people believe that entrepreneurs think, dream and live their business. I also believe that time spent away from the business brings a fresh eye, broadens the horizon and creates new contacts. I never did focus on my business life to the exclusion of all else. Networking

– keeping in touch with the outside world – is an excellent way to find out what is going on.

I always keep tabs on my business, even when I am on business trips. I'm a firm believer that one should never – for any reason – be out of touch with one's business.

> Both of the above paragraphs are true; they are also contradictory. If you are never out of touch with the business, then you are not really spending time away from it. A sad fact of modern technology is that no one needs to be out of touch no matter where they are. Simply unplugging the phone and computer at home can be far more salutary than flying off to the South Seas with your lap-top and cell phone in tow.

Entrepreneurs who have founded and run companies naturally look upon their business enterprises as their own special creations, as if they were their children. You can't run a successful company, however, without eventually loosening the reins, and that's not always easy to do. It feels like letting a beloved child go out into the world, you have to let go, but it is very painful.

> The trick here is to be sure you hand control over to someone you know and trust before it is snatched by some scoundrel.

SELECTING YOUR
MIDDLE MANAGEMENT TEAM

I have always tried to promote from within the company. Choosing associates is a tricky business and I have always trusted character more than education. I like working with people who know the company and have a feel for the way we operate.

> This also gives you a far better insight into the individual than when you hire someone from the outside.

DEALING WITH YOUR
MIDDLE MANAGEMENT TEAM

I never found it hard to hire good managers, but I had to learn how to give them leeway and make sure they used it. I told them, 'Don't expect me to second-guess you. Success or failure is up to you'. There is no point in hiring able people if you don't give them a chance to use their abilities. With the responsibility squarely on their shoulders, people learn to act decisively.

> Remember, one of these people may eventually take your place. Teach them well and let them get as much experience as possible before you move up or out.

My co-workers and I developed a tradition that buoyed us up during long business trips. Every trip, we'd all go out for a special dinner together – just us – to eat the best food and drink the best wine. Then, at the end of the meal, we'd ask the waiter to remove the labels from the wine bottles. Everyone signed the labels and they became mementos of our triumphant forays.

> When you relax with your management team, let them do most of the talking. This allows you not to be the boss, but prevents you from becoming 'just one of the boys'.

DEALING WITH THE WORKFORCE

I measure the success of my efforts by the number of people who have stayed with the company in double digit years. Their loyalty is a matter of great satisfaction and growth.

It may seem premature to prepare an employee manual when you have only a handful of people, but in the long run it will smooth the path for employee relations. Your manual should deal with such issues as vacations, dress code, hours of work and compensation for sick leave.

> Very sound advice and something that far too many small companies, and semi-independent departments in large companies, forget. An employee manual can prevent a lot of misunderstanding. When something comes up that is not covered in the manual, revise the manual to cover it.

You will have to concentrate on finding just the right kinds of employees for your business. While recruiting is time consuming, it is worth the investment.

Don't over-hire. Spend time and effort on training people. In the end, they will appreciate the trouble you have taken to turn them into skilled workers.

> Too many people with overlapping responsibilities is a money pit that can suck you dry in no time. There will never be a need to 'downsize' if you increase your workforce responsibly.

To keep good employees, we offered them tuition reimbursement and four month pregnancy leaves. I instituted those policies because I felt strongly that treating people decently and humanely was the only way to run a good, solid business.

> It is also the only way to keep good employees.

DEALING WITH BUSINESS ASSOCIATES

It didn't take me long to realize that the key to achieving success and minimizing risk lay in having reliable agents and product sources; representatives you can trust.

It isn't just the agents you pick who are important in business. Reliable vendors – the people you buy merchandise from – play an equally decisive role.

> Almost all of us are middlemen: part of a chain. If those on either side of us fall down, it makes us look bad. You can't control the other people in the chain, but, to the greatest extent possible, try to be linked with responsible people.

Think twice before giving your trust to someone and maintain a healthy scepticism at all times.

PUBLIC RELATIONS

You really need to do market research before you start your business. First, decide which segment of the market your product appeals to. . . Match your product to your potential customers. Your advertising must be in line with your product and the market you're targeting. . .

> Decide who will buy your product, or service, and then target your advertising straight at them.

Your customers are the key to the survival of your business. Their responses will keep your company afloat. Therefore, woo them with all your creative energies.

Customer trust makes or breaks you. Above and beyond every other consideration, be honest with your customers. We bend over backwards to make sure that our customers aren't disappointed. But what if, in spite of all the work and effort, orders are late arriving from suppliers and therefore late going out? We do our best to let our customers know what has happened rather than let them stew about their orders. Our policy costs us extra money, but the reassurance it gives the customer is worth it. If a customer returns an item, refund the money as quickly as you can without hesitation. Always remember that without customers, you have no business: repeat customers are the firm foundation of any company. For more than four decades now, many of the same people have continued to order from Lillian Vernon.

> Be honest with your customers, don't equivocate or make excuses. You may lose a sale through no fault of your own, but in the long run they will appreciate your honesty.

From the outset you need to develop your customer database. Once you have built a customer base. . . you must nurture it with care and patience. Record the name and address of everyone who buys from you. . . and, most importantly, what they buy, what they spend and when they re-order. From the beginning of my business until today, I have expended energy and money on my mailing list. Bankers believe that our plant and computer systems are our main assets but they are mistaken. It's our list. Mailing lists are the basic building blocks of our company.

> As important as keeping good customer records is keeping in touch with them. Most businesses that change suppliers or support services do so because those firms fail to make courtesy calls. Out of sight, out of mind.

As your list grows, other companies want to rent your names and list rental can be a significant source of income. I started to rent out lists to other companies and rented names from them, or we traded them. It may seem self-defeating for companies to share their customer lists with their competitors, but that's exactly what happens. When our company rents someone else's list, the first thing we look for is the date of a customer's last order. Current customers are the most desirable.

> Be careful with mailing lists, 'junk mail' is the bane of business and domestic shoppers.

SECTION IV

KINGS, QUEENS AND CONQUERORS

HAMMURABI

King of Babylon, born c.1820 BC, reigned 1792–1750 BC

King of Babylon in the 18th century BC (centuries before Solomon became king of Judea), Hammurabi seems to have been unusually progressive among ancient rulers. Although frequently involved in wars with his neighbours, he successfully brought most of the Mesopotamian city states under a single leadership. . . his own.

To rule his new and expanded empire, Hammurabi developed a code of surprisingly enlightened laws. The laws of Hammurabi must have gained acceptance far beyond the borders of his kingdom, as many of them appear, nearly unchanged, among the laws of Moses in Chapters 21 and 22 of the Book of Exodus. (See our chapter on Moses, p.43, for additional Hebrew laws.)

Despite the fact that Hammurabi imposed the death penalty for an array of civil offences, trial by ordeal and the *lex talionis* (an 'eye for an eye'), the code still represented a significant advance over earlier codes of justice which tended to be imposed with barbaric harshness, or great leniency, depending upon the momentary whim of the king or local judges. Here, for the first time, personal vendettas were outlawed, as were taking wives by capture. Servants, slaves and workers all had to be treated fairly and the no-fault divorce (brought by either the wife or the husband) became an accepted fact of law. Amazingly, ex-husbands were even required to support former wives and children. Hammurabi himself described his work as 'A righteous law, and pious statute'.

Throughout the laws, people who falsely accuse others, or judges who misrule through negligence, are forced to make reparation in equal or greater amount than the damages originally claimed. This sort of approach in today's legal system might dramatically reduce some of the more frivolous cases that clog our court systems. There is also a good management lesson here for those forced to deal with whining and complaining employees.

The complete code contains a total of 282 laws. We have extracted those that apply to modern management techniques, and arranged them under our own topic headings. Obviously, employing any of these rules too literally today is not a good idea!

DEALING WITH THE WORKFORCE

I, Hammurabi, the exalted prince, who feared God, decree these laws to further the well-being of mankind, to bring about the rule of righteousness in the land, to destroy the wicked and the evil-doers; so that the strong should not harm the weak. I, Hammurabi, make riches increase, and bring about the well-being of the oppressed.

> Let everyone know who is the boss and not only how much they owe to him, but also just how much power he has.

If a man is robbed and the robber is not caught, then shall he who was robbed claim under oath the amount of his loss; then shall the community compensate him for the goods stolen.

> Universal, charitable compensation for loss was a standard practice in socially advanced communities and enlightened countries across the globe, until the early years of the 20th century. It provided a sense of security and trust in one's fellows that we have sadly lost and might do well to recapture.

If a chieftain or a common soldier, who has been ordered to go upon the king's highway for war, does not go, but hires a mercenary, if he withholds the compensation then shall this officer or man be put to death, and he who represented him shall take possession of his house.

The time of hiring mercenaries may be long over, but a similar rule could well apply to those who refuse to pay an employee for their services or deal unfairly with subcontractors or freelancers.

If anyone leaves his house, runs away, and then his wife goes to another house; if then he returns, and wishes to take his wife back, because he fled from his home and ran away, the wife of this runaway shall not return to her husband.

It may not be business, but it is a surprisingly enlightened view of the independent position of women in Babylon nearly four thousand years ago.

CORPORATE THEFT AND CRIME

If anyone bring an accusation of any crime before the elders, and does not prove what he has charged, he shall, if it be a capital offence charged, be put to death.

The punishment may seem a bit harsh, but the seriousness of false accusations and rumour campaigns should not be underestimated.

If anyone steal the property of a temple, or of the court, he shall be put to death, and also the one who receives the stolen thing from him shall be put to death.

In modern terms, anyone caught stealing from the company, no matter how small the theft, should be fined.

If anyone steal cattle or sheep, or an ass, or a pig or a goat, if it belong to a god or to the court, the thief shall pay 30 fold therefore; if they belonged to a free man he shall pay ten fold; if the thief has nothing with which to pay he shall be put to death.

An interesting deterrent to industrial espionage and theft of intellectual property!

If anyone has a consignment of corn or money, and he take from the granary or box without the knowledge of the owner, then shall he who took corn without the knowledge of the owner out of the granary, or money out of the box, be legally convicted and repay the corn he has taken. And he shall lose whatever commission was paid to him, or due him.

A perfectly fair and equitable punishment for corporate theft.

If a man put out the eye of another man, his eye shall be put out.
If he break another man's bone, his bone shall be broken.
If a man knock out the teeth of his equal, his teeth shall be knocked out.
If any one strike the body of a man higher in rank than he, he shall receive 60 blows with an ox-whip in public.

The above four laws have a distinctly Old Testament 'eye for an eye' flavour to them, but realistically, in-kind compensation for damages is not a bad idea for private or corporate property. In personal situations, however, it would prove massively unpopular, if not illegal.

LEGAL PROCEDURE

If he satisfy the elders to impose a fine of grain or money, he shall receive the fine that the action produces.

In all probability this means no exorbitant court costs or lawyers' fees that can be devoured by 'the system'.

Following a short set of rules governing the prices that a physician may charge for his services, is this:

If a physician make a large incision with the operating knife, and kill him, or open a tumour with the operating knife, and cut out the eye, his hands shall be cut off.

An interesting alternative to suing for malpractice!

DEALING WITH BUSINESS ASSOCIATES

If anyone give another silver, gold or anything else to keep, he shall show everything to some witness, draw up a contract and then hand it over for safe keeping.

Good business practices never change. Drawing up a contract, even an adversarial one, does not imply mistrust, it simply acknowledges the impartiality of contract law.

If he turn it over for safe keeping without witness or contract, and if he to whom it was given deny it, then he has no legitimate claim.

Just as good business practices remain unaltered, so does common sense. Always get a contract or receipt for any exchange of goods or services.

If anyone buy from the son or the slave of another man, without witnesses or a contract, silver or gold, a male or female slave, an ox or a sheep, an ass or anything, or if he take it in charge, he is considered a thief and shall be put to death.

A serious admonition to determine the source of goods purchased. This could keep your company out of trouble should the goods prove to be stolen.

If a merchant entrust money to an agent for some investment, and the broker suffer a loss in the place to which he goes, he shall make good the capital to the merchant.

An interesting approach to investment policy but not one likely to be willingly adopted by your investment house.

If a merchant cheat his sales representative, in that as the latter has returned to him all the money that had been entrusted to him, but the merchant denies the receipt of the returned money, then shall this agent convict the merchant before God and the judges, and if he still deny receiving what the agent had given him shall pay six times the sum to the agent.

Not cheating someone who is acting in good faith on your behalf is no more than common sense. Here the policy is given teeth.

MANAGING A SUBSIDIARY COMPANY

If a chieftain or soldier leave his house, garden and field and hires it out, and someone else takes possession of his house, garden and field and uses it for three years: if the first owner return and claims his house, garden and field, it shall not be given to him, but he who has taken possession of it and used it shall continue to use it.

A strong admonition against absentee ownership.

If a man rent his field for tillage for a fixed rental, and receive the rent of his field, but bad weather comes and destroys the harvest, the injury falls upon the tiller of the soil.

A valid consideration: the risk of business lies solely on the head of a business tenant or franchise holder.

If anyone owe a debt for a loan, and a storm prostrates the grain, or the harvest fail, or the grain does not grow for lack of water; in that year he need not give his creditor any grain, he washes his debt-tablet in water and pays no rent for this year.

This seems to contradict the previous law, but it may be seen as a plea for leniency in cases where a business tenant or franchise holder suffers early losses through no fault of his own.

If a tenant farmer has no money to repay, then he shall pay in corn or sesame in place of the money as rent for what he received from the merchant, according to the royal tariff.

Paying in kind, rather than in hard cash, is always a viable option and one that may prevent both parties from long and unpleasant legal battles.

If a man transform waste land into arable fields and return it to its owner, the latter shall pay him for one year ten gur (a measure of grain) for ten gan (an area of land).

An exceptionally equitable approach to lease-hold improvement, but not one likely to prove popular with landlords.

SOLOMON

King of Judea, mid-10th century BC

Referring to someone as having the 'wisdom of Solomon' has almost become a cliché, but the fact remains that Solomon was a wise and clever ruler. He transformed the scattered tribes of Israel into a nation by creating administrative subdivisions that crossed traditional tribal boundaries. This effectively removed tribal independence and kept the power where it belonged: in Solomon's palace.

With his people living in forced unity, Solomon set out to destroy his enemies, both those within his own nation and those, such as the Philistines, whose empires were within easy striking distance of Solomon's country, Judea. Within his own country, Solomon destroyed his enemies by court intrigue; and despite developing his army to world class standards, he was clever enough to avoid battle wherever possible.

To cement alliances with established allies, potential allies and potential enemies that he wanted to convert to friends, Solomon joined the family. . . literally. He had, according to the Old Testament book of I. Kings, in excess of 700 wives and nearly 300 concubines.

Outside the walls of Jerusalem, his capital city, he built shrines to the pagan gods worshipped by the hundreds of foreign visitors who flocked to Jerusalem as diplomats and merchants; this way they knew they were welcome in the Hebrew capital.

In addition to being a clever leader and administrator, Solomon was regarded as an accessible and phenomenally wise judge, even to the point of having supernatural powers. According to the *Arabian Nights*, it was Solomon who imprisoned the evil Genie in the bottle. The king himself, however, modestly attributed his wisdom to God rather than to himself. In I. Kings, Chapter 3, verse 9, Solomon prays: 'Give therefore thy servant an understanding heart to judge Thy people, that I may discern between good and bad. . .'

The main story, below, is also taken from I. Kings, Chapter 3, and it is probably the most frequently quoted example of how Solomon was able to separate truth from lies. It is worth noting that the women involved are harlots (prostitutes) who were outcasts in traditional Hebrew society; yet they were granted access to no less than the king himself. Their trade also tells us that the child involved in the case is almost undoubtedly illegitimate, a terrible stigma, but again it makes no difference to Solomon. He is not judging the women's morality, nor their crime of prostitution (which carried a sentence of death by stoning), but only their civil suit. The story is offered here in its entirety, exactly as it appears in the Old Testament, but with our modern-day topic heading.

SETTLING PERSONNEL DISPUTES

(I. Kings:3)

16 Then came there two women, that were harlots, unto the king, and stood before him.

17 And one woman said, 'O my lord, I and this woman dwell in one house; and I was delivered of a child with her in the house.

18 And it came to pass that the third day after I was delivered, that this woman was delivered also: and we were together; there was no stranger with us in the house. . .

19 And this woman's child died in the night; because she overlaid it (rolled over on top of it).

20 And she arose at midnight, and took my son from beside me, while I slept, and laid it in her bosom, and laid her dead child in my bosom.

21 And when I arose in the morning to give my child suck, behold it was dead: but when I had considered it in the morning light behold, it was not my son. . .'

22 And the other woman said, 'Nay; but the living is my son, and the dead is thy son'. And the first said, 'No; but the dead is thy son, and the living is my son'. Thus they spake before the king.

23 Then said the king, 'The one sayeth "This is my son that liveth, and thy son is dead" and the other sayeth, "Nay; but thy son is the dead and my son is the living."'

24 And the king said, 'Bring me a sword'. And they brought a sword before the king.

25 And the king said, 'Divide the living child in two, and give half to the one and half to the other.'

26 Then spake the woman whose the living child truly was to the king, for her heart yearned upon her son, and she said, 'O my lord, give her the living child and in no way slay it.' But the other said 'Let it be neither mine nor thine, but divide it.'

27 Then the king answered and said: 'Give her the living child and in no wise slay it; she is truly the mother thereof.'

28 And all Israel heard the judgement which the king had judged; and they feared the king for they saw that the wisdom of God was in him to do judgement.

> Obviously, without having appeared to do so, what Solomon has done is judged the women themselves. The real mother would probably be far more concerned with the life of the child than securing its possession; and even if she were not, the woman who had the most concern for the child would undoubtedly be the most suitable candidate for nurturing the baby. Sometimes it is more important to make the wise choice than to make the technically correct one.

In addition to carrying out this feat of judicial wisdom, Solomon was probably the author of the book of Proverbs. We have selected a few verses from Proverbs that seem appropriate to business dealings and included them below. They do not appear here in the same order they do in the Bible, but have been grouped by topic under our headings. The text, however, remains unaltered.

DEALING WITH SUPERIORS

(17:11) An evil man seeketh only rebellion: therefore a cruel messenger shall be sent against him.

> Anyone who stirs up trouble can expect to be paid back in kind, but it will probably be worse when it comes back around.

(26:4) Answer not a fool according to his own folly, lest thou also be like unto him.

> Don't let anyone, either a superior or those in your charge, goad you into losing your temper even, or especially, if they have lost theirs. This will

only make a bad situation worse and you will end up being as much at fault as they are.

BECOMING AN EFFECTIVE MANAGER

(8:11) For wisdom is better than rubies; and all the things that are to be desired are not to be compared to it.

(11:29) He that troubleth his own house shall inherit the wind.

Don't stir up trouble in the office, in the company or at home; and disassociate yourself from anyone foolish enough do so.

(16:18) Pride goeth before destruction, and an haughty spirit before a fall.

Never allow yourself to get complacent. The minute you start to think you are unassailable, you let your guard down and some hungry upstart will come along and devour you.

(18:13) He that answereth a matter before he heareth it, it is folly and shame unto him.

Never jump to conclusions and never assume anything. Unless you can verify it, the chances are that the scary rumour, whatever it is, is just that, a rumour. If you believe it and panic, you will probably be embarrassed later. If you actually act on it you could end up in deep trouble.

(22:3) A prudent man forseeth evil, and hideth himself: but the simple pass on and are punished.

Almost in contradiction to the previous proverb, but no less true. A well developed ability to read your 'gut feelings' is essential to survival in the world of business. It is what keeps the winners one step ahead of everyone else.

(22:28) Remove not the ancient landmark which thy fathers have set.

> From the late 1960s until the end of the 1980s, 'change for the sake of change' seems to have been one of business's basic tenets. A lot of survivors, not to mention a lot of victims, from that era regret their hasty actions. After a decade or so of promotions, retirements and funerals, the lessons are likely to be forgotten. Too bad.

(24:28) Be not a witness against thy neighbour without cause; and deceive not with thy lips.

> Don't gossip and don't lie. No one has a good enough memory to succeed at it forever.

(29:18) Where there is no vision, the people perish: but he that keepeth the law, happy is he.

> It is essential to have vision and forethought if you are going to succeed. Most people just blunder along dealing with life from crisis to crisis. True vision will put you miles ahead of the competition.

DEALING WITH YOUR MIDDLE MANAGEMENT TEAM

(22:29) See thou a man diligent in his business? He shall stand before kings; he shall not stand before petty men.

> Hard work elevates a person to a very special group of people. When one of your management team does a particularly good job, reward them.

(3:27) Withhold not good from them to whom it is due, when it is in the power of thine hand to do it.

> Whenever possible reward your people personally. Even if it is just a good word, if it comes directly from you it can provide a greater moral boost than an award that comes down from some faceless office.

(11:14) Where no council is, the people fall: but in the multitude of councillors there is safety.

> This advises not only to keep your people informed and instructed on what is expected of them, but also to be sure all of your management do the same and are in absolute agreement on procedure. Conflicting orders are one of the commonest sources of complaint in companies.

(14:17) He that is soon angry dealeth foolishly; and a man of wicked devices is hated.

> People who are unable to control their temper will quickly earn a bad reputation and no one will want to work with them. This will quickly put them out of the information loop and, eventually, out of a job.

(14:29) He that is slow to wrath is of great understanding: but he that is hasty of spirit exalteth folly.

> Pretty much an extension of the above. Those who berate people for minor mistakes are causing themselves more problems than they are solving.

(15:1) A soft answer turneth away wrath: but grievous words stir up anger.

> This is pretty self-explanatory. Don't jump all over your people. Even if they make a mistake, dealing with them quietly and reasonably will get you a lot further than shouting at them.

(23:13) Withhold not correction from the child, for if thou beatest him with the rod, he shall not die.

> This again is fairly obvious. Don't be afraid to discipline your employees when necessary. It won't kill them. They might learn something and it will reinforce your position of authority.

(25:19) Having confidence in an unfaithful man in a time of trouble is as painful as a broken tooth or a foot out of joint.

Don't rely on gossips and spies to back you up. When you need them they will disappear.

(26:6) He that entrusteth a message to the hand of a fool, cutteth off his own feet.

Clarification is hardly needed here.

(26:11) As a dog returneth to his own vomit, so a fool returns to his folly.

A rather earthy continuation of several of the above. Once an employee establishes a pattern of lazy, deceitful or downright dishonest behaviour, chances are they are going to repeat it. Watch them like a hawk.

(28:13) He that covereth his sins shall not prosper: but whoso confesseth and forsaketh his ways shall have mercy.

Sometimes people do stupid things. If one of yours does, confront them with the facts. If they are honest enough and admit what they did, let it slide as reasonably as possible. If they try to lie their way out of it, watch out, you may have a much bigger problem on your hands.

(29:20) Seest thou a man who is hasty in his words; there is more hope for a fool than for him.

'Hot headed' and 'lacking discretion' should not be words to describe members of your management team.

DEALING WITH THE WORKFORCE

(3:31) Envy not the oppressor, and choose none of his ways.

Abusive use of power may look very appealing. In fact, like a deal with the devil, it inevitably leads to disaster.

(18:9) He also that is slothful in his work is brother to him that is a great waster.

Lackadaisical employees, or those who are just plain lazy, can breed bad feelings among workers amazingly quickly. Everyone resents a bad worker but many of them will emulate the lout because they feel that if one person can get away with it so can everybody else. These people cost you money; deal with them accordingly.

(19:5) A false witness shall not be unpunished, and he that speaketh lies shall not escape.

Liars and malicious gossips can cause more bad feelings in the work environment than almost any other sort of trouble, except an imminent takeover. If you suspect something like this is going on, try to isolate it and deal with the perpetrator quickly and firmly.

(26:24) He that is filled with hate, dissembleth with his lips and layeth up deceit within him.

Employees who constantly have a chip on their shoulder will inevitably end up being trouble-makers. Isolate them or, if possible, have them transferred to another department. It will save you a lot of grief later on.

(27:23) Be thou diligent to know the state of thy flocks, and look well to thy herds.

Look after people in your charge, both managers and employees; knowing their names and the names of their spouses and children can be a great aid to good relations and it costs nothing.

DEALING WITH BUSINESS ASSOCIATES

(10:18) He that hideth hatred with lying lips, and he that uttereth a slander, is a fool.

Beware the hypocrite and the gossip. If they will do it to someone else, they will do it to you.

(11:13) A carrier of tales revealeth secrets; but he that is of a faithful spirit concealeth the matter.

Never trust someone who gives you inside information. They have betrayed someone's confidence already, there is no reason why they won't betray yours as well. When someone refuses to supply information 'to' you, do not accuse them of withholding information or turning against you. It may simply be that they have a strong moral code. At least you will have the satisfaction of knowing that it is unlikely they will supply someone else with information 'about' you!

(13:3) He that keepeth his mouth shut keepeth his life: but he that openeth wide his lips shall have destruction.

Discretion is often the better part of valour. Don't associate with blabber mouths.

(22:7) The rich ruleth over the poor: and the borrower is servant to the lender.

In the same way the boss will always be the boss, anyone who has a direct line into your pocket will also be able to control you. Debt may be inevitable but, despite what the 'leveraged buy-out kings' say, it will never be your friend.

(22:24) Make no friendship with an angry man; and with a furious man thou shalt not go.

(24:1-2) Be thou not envious of evil men, neither desire to be with them. For their heart studieth destruction and their lips talk of mischief.

Don't worry because some unscrupulous toad nudged ahead of you. Even if you never quite catch up with them, at least you don't have to spend your life looking over your shoulder.

(25:17) Withdraw thy foot from thy neighbour's house; lest he be wary of thee, and so hate thee.

Don't interfere in other people's business, be it office politics or the business of another firm. In the long run it will engender more bad blood than advancement.

(25:28) He that hath no rule over his own spirit is like a city that is broken down and without walls.

Beware of dealing with loose cannons, there is no defence against them.

(27:6) Faithful are the wounds of a friend, but the kisses of an enemy are deceitful.

Painful as it may be at the time, you will be a lot better off listening to a friend telling you when you have gone wrong than listening to someone who will encourage you to continue on a course of disaster. Harder still, but just as important, is to be the friend who has to confront someone they care about and straighten them out.

(28:10) Whoso causeth the righteous to go astray in an evil way, he shall fall himself into his own pit: but the upright shall have good things in possession.

Whether by enticement, bribe or blackmail, undermining a good person is a one-way ticket to disaster. Avoid people who engage in such practices.

(29:11) A fool uttereth all his mind; but a wise man keepeth it in till afterwards.

Think much, say little. When you do speak, let it be only to those you trust implicitly.

(29:5) A man that flattereth his neighbour spreadeth a net for his feet.

Flattery is a drug; the more you get, the more you want. Like all drugs it comes at a high price and will inevitably cloud your judgement.

DEALING WITH THE COMPETITION

(22:16) He that oppresseth the poor to increase his riches. . . shall surely come to want.

Don't take advantage of another business just because it is vulnerable. It might make you money but it will also make you look like a bully and eventually even those who once respected your business acumen will start to avoid you.

KING JOHN

King of England, born 1167, reigned 1199–1216

Despite being one of the most notorious figures in English history, King John remains personally something of an enigma. There is little doubt his reign was unhappy, both for England and for John himself. His mother, the wilful and overbearing Eleanor of Aquitaine, called him 'inconstant'; William Marshall, his military advisor, said he had 'a heart of wax'. Others were less flattering!

John initially came to the throne in 1189, not as king but as care-taker for his brother Richard (the Lionheart) who spent most of his ten-year reign merrily making war across Europe and the Holy Land. This left John to keep the nobility in line and raise endless taxes to fund his brother's expeditions, without having any real power of enforcement. Had he been as cruel as he is portrayed in the Robin Hood legends, he might have been more successful than he was. But John tried to deal with the barons as individuals, making different, often conflicting, deals with each one.

Inevitably, John became known as someone who made promises he could not, or would not, keep. It may be that John wanted to be a strong leader and still have people like him. He never learned that the two are virtually incompatible for someone in a position of power. By promising different barons different things at different times, John did little more than ensure that everyone mistrusted him.

When Richard died in 1199 and John came to the throne in his own right, he passed laws restoring the power of the monarchy. Faced with losing their wayward lifestyle, the barons threatened to go to war. Faced with far too many enemies to deal with, John relented. In 1215 a hurried series of negotiations took place in which the king and the barons cobbled together an agreement that would forever change how the kings of England would rule. That agreement is known as the Magna Carta – the Great Charter – and is, in effect, the world's first constitutional guarantee of rights.

The greatest lesson here may lie in the flawed life of King John himself. Never allow yourself to be placed in a position where your authority relies on making concessions and impractical promises which strip away your authority.

Below are selected passages from the Magna Carta that have practical application to modern business. The passages have been edited and rearranged for clarity and consistency under our topic headings.

PREAMBLE

John, by the Grace of God, King of England, Lord of Ireland, Duke of Normandy and Aquitaine, and Count of Anjou, to his archbishops,

bishops, abbots, earls, barons, justices, foresters, sheriffs, stewards, servants, and to all his officials and loyal subjects, greeting.

> Even though he is signing the charter under duress, John sets out his complete list of titles to emphasize the fact that he is still king. There follows a list of 27 men who helped word the charter, both on behalf of the king and in opposition to him. Publicly attaching people's names to a radical document is a double-edged sword. While it certainly establishes their importance in the 'new order of things' it also makes them responsible, and accountable, for any problems arising from the execution of the new laws.

MANAGEMENT AND WORKER RIGHTS AND RESPONSIBILITIES

First, that we have granted to God by this present charter, and have confirmed for us and our heirs in perpetuity, that the English Church shall be free, and shall have its rights undiminished and its liberties unimpaired. That we wish this so to be observed, appears from the fact that of our own free will, before the outbreak of the present dispute between us and our barons, we granted and confirmed by charter the freedom of the Church's elections – a right reckoned to be of the greatest necessity and importance to it – and caused this to be confirmed by Pope Innocent III. This freedom we shall observe ourselves, and desire to be observed in good faith by our heirs in perpetuity. We have also granted to all free men of our realm, for us and our heirs for ever, all the liberties written out below, to have and to keep for them and their heirs, by us and our heirs.

> This section of the text guarantees the freedom of the Church, the medieval equivalent of guaranteeing freedom of religion and prohibiting minority discrimination. While such things are not normally set out in major

company policy it is certainly good public relations. While there is no sure guarantee against personal prejudices, this at least guarantees that no such biases are institutionalized.

The Church always insisted on holding their own elections for the church hierarchy. Similarly, workers' organizations and unions need to be assured that their elections will not be controlled or influenced by corporate management.

The final sentence guarantees that the statutes are intended to be inviolate and to stand in perpetuity. Obviously nothing lasts forever, but there is a nice sense of security in believing they might. In reality this is little more than a 'feel good' factor, but it is good press.

The guardian of the land of an heir who is under age shall take from it only reasonable revenues, customary dues and feudal services. He shall do this without destruction or damage to men or property. If we have given or sold to anyone the guardianship of such land, and he causes destruction or damage, he shall lose the guardianship of it and it shall be handed over to two worthy and prudent men of the same parish who shall be similarly answerable to us.

For so long as a guardian has guardianship of such land, he shall maintain the houses, parks, fish preserves, ponds, mills and everything else pertaining to it, from the revenues of the land itself.

This sets out the rights and responsibilities of middle management, in this case the barons and the lords who control the peasant workers. Middle management are strictly prohibited from abusing people or property under their control and are to be held personally liable if they overstep the prescribed limits of their power. These two paragraphs also make them responsible for seeing that the next generation of workers are treated fairly and are not cheated of their future source of income. Talent should always be protected and promoted.

To obtain the general consent of the realm for the assessment of tax, we will cause the archbishops, bishops, abbots, earls and greater barons to be summoned individually by letter. To those who hold lands directly from us, we will cause a general summons to be issued, through the sheriffs and other officials, to come together on a fixed day (of which at least 40 days' notice shall be given) and at a fixed place. In all letters of summons, the cause of the summons will be stated. When a summons has been issued, the business appointed for the day shall go forward in accordance with the resolution of those present, even if not all those who were summoned have appeared.

> Here is a guarantee that no changes of policy will take place without the notification of advisors, stockholders and middle management. This not only gives those responsible for the day-to-day running of the company the security of knowing they are 'in the loop', but also ensures that they are aware of any changes in policy they are expected to implement, thus removing the excuse that they were not aware of the policy changes in question.

In future we will allow no one to levy a tax from his free men, except to ransom his person, to make his eldest son a knight and to marry his eldest daughter. For these purposes only a reasonable tax may be levied.

> This clause, an extension of the one above, ensures that middle management do not overstep their bounds. It also prohibits them from making rules that overstep those approved by corporate heads, or act in contradiction of company policy.

No constable or other bailiff of ours shall take the corn or other chattels of anyone except he straightway give money for them, or can be allowed a respite in that regard by the will of the seller.

No sheriff nor bailiff of ours, nor any one else, shall take the horses or carts of any free man for transport, unless by the will of that free man.

Neither we nor our bailiffs shall take another's wood for castles or for other private uses, unless by the will of him to whom the wood belongs.

> These three paragraphs ensure that private property, or the product of an individual's labour, remain inviolate. This is particularly relevant today, when ownership of intellectual property is so often a matter of dispute. This section guarantees that the fruits of an employee's labour, created on their own time, belong to them alone.

We will not make men justices, constables, sheriffs or bailiffs unless they are such as know the law of the realm, and are minded to observe it rightly.

> This is a simple assurance of appointing qualified managers and supervisors. Particularly in situations where new management takes over, there are inevitable worker concerns about nepotism or the introduction of people from outside the company who, if not actually unqualified, are at least unfamiliar with the established way of doing things.

And straightway after peace is restored we shall remove from the realm all the foreign soldiers, crossbowmen, servants and hirelings who may have come with horses and arms to the harm of the realm.

> Like the paragraph above, this alludes to the importation of outside people. Here, however, we are dealing not with permanent managers but the temporary hirelings whose presence so often means a spot of 'house cleaning' is about to take place. Efficiency experts, management consultants and others are often seen as being brought in to eliminate jobs and rearrange comfortable working conditions. The presence of such consultants may indicate that management has not kept a tight reign on the company and is about to compound one mistake with another.

SETTLING PERSONNEL DISPUTES

Inquests. . . shall be taken only in their proper county court. We ourselves, or in our absence abroad our chief justice, will send two justices to each county four times a year, and these justices, with four knights of the county elected by residents of the county itself, shall hold court, within the boundary of the county, on the day and in the place where the court normally meets.

> This establishes a regular system of arbitration, leaving no doubt that personnel grievances will be dealt with. It also establishes particular times when such hearings will take place, thus eliminating constant agitation to convene boards of arbitration or inquiry that are only called as needed.

Inasmuch as, for the sake of God, and the bettering of our realm, and for the more ready healing of the discord which has arisen between us and our barons, we have made all these aforesaid concessions. . . wishing our subjects to enjoy forever a stable government, we make and grant to them the following security:

The barons may elect, from among themselves, 25 men who ought, with all their strength, to observe, maintain and cause to be observed, the peace and privileges which we have granted to them and confirmed by this charter.

> This extract sets out the nature of the arbitration board. Here, all the members are from among the nobility, but in modern practice the number should come from both middle management and the workforce. It is always best if upper management stay out of dispensing justice in the workplace. At least if the judgement is unpopular, the boss's hands are clean; if, on the other hand, the arbitration board proves popular, top management can take credit for setting it up.

Earls and barons shall not be judged save by their peers, and only according to the measure of the offence.

Here we take up the controversial question of who is allowed to judge middle management accused of an offence against the company or its employees. Because the Magna Carta was largely written by the barons, they are protected from being tried in common courts. But it is always difficult to decide whether representatives of rank and file employees should have a say in disciplinary actions against management personnel.

All fines imposed by us unjustly and contrary to the law of the land, and all fines that have been extracted unjustly, and contrary to the law of the land, shall be altogether remitted, or it shall be done with regard to them according to the judgement of the 25 barons set out as sureties for the peace, or according to the judgement of the majority of them together with the aforesaid Stephen, Archbishop of Canterbury, if he can be present, and with others whom he may wish to associate with himself for this purpose. And if he cannot be present, the affair shall nevertheless proceed without him; in such way that, if one or more of the said 25 barons shall be concerned in a similar complaint, they shall be removed from this particular decision and, in their place, for this purpose alone, others shall be substituted who shall be chosen and sworn by the remainder of those 25.

This ensures that all arbitration and hearing boards will be consistent and completely impartial, even addressing the problem of redressing past injustices. Note that conflicts of interest are dealt with in the last sentence, where any of the arbitration board accused of offences similar to those of the person being heard will be removed from the proceedings.

No bailiff, on his own simple assertion, shall henceforth place anyone before the law without producing faithful witnesses in evidence.

Controlling malicious gossip is always a problem. By ensuring that no one can be dragged before a disciplinary board without evidence, the destructive power of gossip can be, if not eliminated, at least controlled.

To none will we sell, to none deny or delay, the right of justice.

> There has always been the fear that people higher up the social structure get preferential treatment when they cross the line. If staff are going to have faith in top management there must be no suspicion that management wrongs are punished with less severity than those of the general workforce.

FINANCIAL DEALINGS

For a trivial offence, a free man shall be fined only in proportion to the degree of his offence, and for a serious offence correspondingly, but not so heavily as to deprive him of his livelihood. In the same way, a merchant shall be spared his merchandise, and a husbandman the implements of his husbandry, if they fall upon the mercy of a royal court. None of these fines shall be imposed except by the assessment on oath of reputable men of the neighbourhood.

> Under no circumstances shall anyone be so encumbered by debt or fine that they are unable to make their living. Far too often people pledge their entire means of livelihood as security for a loan. This not only cautions that you should not allow yourself to get into this situation, but also not to allow others to endebt themselves to you in such a way that they might be ruined if they cannot fulfil the terms of the debt.

Neither we nor our officials will seize any land or rent in payment of a debt, so long as the debtor has moveable goods sufficient to discharge the debt. A debtor's sureties shall not be distrained upon so long as the debtor himself can discharge his debt. If, for lack of means, the debtor is unable to discharge his debt, his sureties shall be answerable for it. If they so desire, they may have the debtor's lands and rents until they have received satisfaction for the debt that they paid for him, unless the debtor can show that he has settled his obligations to them.

Like the item above, this deals with security for a business loan and how far to push a debtor unable to repay a loan. Here, the solution is the temporary confiscation of land and business property, but only until the debt is paid off.

If anyone who has borrowed a sum of money dies before the debt has been repaid, his heir shall pay no interest on the debt for so long as he remains under age, irrespective of in whose name he holds his lands. If such a debt falls into the hands of the Crown, it will take nothing except the principal sum specified in the bond.

Again, there is a real attempt not to bankrupt a debtor, in this case, someone who has inherited a debt. Here, the solution to an inherited debt is amazingly fair. Only the remaining principal on the loan is collectable. Any remaining interest being considered to have died along with the original debtor.

MANAGING A SUBSIDIARY COMPANY

The city of London shall enjoy all its ancient liberties and free customs, both by land and by water. We also will and grant that all other cities, boroughs, towns and ports shall enjoy all their liberties and free customs.

In effect, this ensures that when a new corporate government takes control of a company there will be no changes in policy adversely affecting the way the satellite company operates. It is a good policy to allow wholly-owned or subsidiary companies to retain their traditional ways of doing business. It reassures them that the new owners, or the management of the parent company, will not interfere with their business or their ability to make a profit.

No man shall be forced to perform more service for a knight's fee, or other free holding of land, than is due from it.

> Designed to prevent the sale of land and titles of nobility for more than their actual value, this law can, and should, be applied to business in general. No one should ever be induced to take on more debt load than the business used as security can bear. To anyone not familiar with the curious ways of major takeovers this would seem obvious to the point of stupidity, but far too frequently successful businesses have been sold off piece by piece, in the name of stockholder profit, to rid the company of an unsupportable debt load.

If we have deprived or dispossessed Welshmen of their lands or liberties or other things without legal judgement of their peers, in England or in Wales. . . they shall straightway be restored to them. And if a dispute shall arise concerning this, then action shall be taken upon it through judgement of their peers. . . concerning English holdings according to the law of England, concerning Welsh holdings according to the law of Wales. The Welsh shall do likewise with regard to us and our subjects.

> If we consider Wales as a subsidiary of England, this law makes an interesting point on determining company policy in subsidiary branches. Here, disputed company policy affecting subsidiaries will be settled by the laws and customs of the subsidiary in question, rather than those of the parent company.

CLOSING

Moreover all the subjects of our realm, clergy as well as laity, shall, as far as pertains to them, observe all the customs that we have granted to them, with regard to their vassals.

This simply states that everyone, regardless of their position in the company, are to be bound by the corporate laws.

Wherefore we will and firmly decree that the English Church shall be free, and that the subjects of our realm shall have and hold all the aforesaid liberties, rights and concessions, duly and in peace, freely and quietly, fully and entirely, for themselves and their heirs from us and our heirs, in all matters and in all places, forever.

By reiterating the basic tenets of the preamble, particularly the part insisting that these laws are permanent and inviolable, the charter is given a sense of having more power than it actually has. Obviously any agreement is only as good as the intentions of the signatories, but people like to feel safe and if you, as the boss, can make them feel safe and secure, all the better for worker–management relations.

Given through our hand, in the plain called Runnymede between Windsor and Stanes, on the fifteenth day of June, in the seventeenth year of our reign.

KING EDWARD I

꒷꒰ꔷ

King of England, born 1239, reigned 1272–1307

England's King Edward I, popularly known as 'longshanks' because of his spectacular height, has been portrayed by contemporaries and historians alike as a hard man. He probably was. Accomplishing any significant change in the often brutal, medieval world required amazing courage and a near-fanatical sense of purpose, both of which Edward possessed in abundance.

In 1272 Edward inherited a kingdom awash with violence. Petty

barons warred among themselves for land and power, while neighbouring Wales and Scotland had been in constant border wars with
England for centuries. Scotland in particular was racked with constant
fighting among clan leaders, each of whom sought to gain the Scottish
throne, mostly by violence. The Scottish wars often involved incursions
into English territory, which were a constant drain on the crown's
resources. It was a situation Edward found intolerable and he set out
to stop it the only way he knew – in battle. He believed the kingdom
would be far better ruled by a single monarch, himself. The concept
of an 'unfriendly takeover' would have been nothing new to Edward
Longshanks. His campaigns to create the first unified Britain earned
him the nickname 'Hammer of the Scots'.

Although his methods might be seen as brutal by today's standards,
Edward was a clever politician and an enlightened ruler. He was always
willing to compromise as long as it was to his long-term advantage,
and every move was carefully built on the rights and responsibilities
that had been set out in the Magna Carta (see our chapter on King
John and the Magna Carta, p.118).

Always an innovator, Edward tried to give something back in
exchange for every concession he demanded from his subjects. He
agreed to make no new laws without calling a parliament to hear the
opinions of his barons. He did not necessarily take their advice, but he
was careful never to appear to act without having considered their
counsel. In exchange for listening to the barons' advice, Edward
stripped them of their traditional right to wear swords and armour in
parliament chambers. It may seem symbolic by today's standards, but
in the 13th century it was a severe blow to the macho mentality of a
warrior class.

In an effort to placate the tempestuous Welsh he incorporated their
longbowmen into his own army. This was calculated to give the Welsh
a sense of being part of England and cleverly provided Edward with
the most terrifyingly effective weapon on the medieval battlefield.

Throughout all this political manoeuvring Edward never lost sight of his long-term goals, most of which centred around keeping his quarrelsome barons in line, suppressing the troublesome Scots and securing the English Crown as the unquestioned centre of power. To this end, he personally dealt with every law no matter how small: from establishing requirements for local coroners to defining the exact nature of treason. Over the course of his 35-year reign Edward enacted more laws than all his predecessors put together. Significantly, Edward made sure that the laws applied to everyone equally; nobility, knights, merchants and peasants were all equally answerable, and woe to anyone who refused to recognize the authority of the king's judges. This seemingly logical step provided the dual advantage of making the baronage answerable for their actions and giving the commoners the assurance that they were not being ignored by their king. Where local or circuit courts alone could not settle a dispute, the king himself was often willing to act as arbitrator, but only when absolutely necessary.

One episode in Edward's battle to gain control over his barons and Scotland has been popularized, and grossly distorted, by Hollywood. He did indeed, fight against, capture and brutally execute, the insurgent leader William Wallace. Wallace, regardless of his sentiments, owed allegiance to the English Crown, and had betrayed his oath of loyalty and become a traitor by taking up arms against his king. Legitimate leaders of the Scots, such as Robert Bruce, frequently held meetings with Edward to discuss possible terms and truces; but Edward would not conscience traitors who operated in defiance of Crown law. It was this, not Wallace's stand against Edward, that led to his grotesque public execution of being hanged, drawn and quartered.

Edward's ability to lead his own troops into battle, to delegate authority, and his willingness to take ultimate responsibility for all his actions, was exceptional.

The statutes following have been taken out of chronological order, edited for clarity and rearranged under our topic headings.

MANAGEMENT AND WORKER
RIGHTS AND RESPONSIBILITIES

Edward, by the Grace of God, King of England, Lord of Ireland and Duke of Guian, to all those that these present letters shall hear or see, Greeting. Know ye that we, to the honour of God, and of Holy Church, and to the profit of our realm, have granted for us and our heirs that the Great Charter of Liberties and the Charter of the Forest, which were made by common assent of all the realm. . . shall be kept in every point without breach. And we [command] that the same charters shall be sent under our seal, to our justices. . . and to all sheriffs. . . and to all our other officers, and to all our cities throughout the realm. . . [and] that they cause the aforesaid charters to be published, and to declare to the people that we have confirmed them in all points. And we [command] that the same charters shall be sent, under our seal, to Cathedral Churches throughout our realm, there to remain, and shall be read before the people two times each year. And that all the Archbishops and Bishops shall pronounce the Sentence of Excommunication against all those that by word, deed or counsel do contrary to the aforesaid charters, or that in any point break or undo them. And that the said curses be twice a year denounced by the prelates aforesaid.

> Edward has made three very smart moves here. First, he promises to abide by the Magna Carta (here referred to as the Great Charter of Liberties); as a newly appointed manager, never let people think you are going to upset their world. Even if you plan to make big changes, don't upset the workers until you have had time to settle in. Secondly, note that he guarantees everyone equal knowledge of the law. No one can accuse you of hiding anything if you put it all out in the open from the start. Finally, Edward commands that the Church excommunicate anyone found guilty of subverting Crown law, be they commoner or nobility. By appealing to a neutral third party arbitrator, you can always keep your hands clean,

even when you have to get rid of troublesome workers or middle management.

First the King wills and commands that the Peace of Holy Church and of the land be well kept and maintained in all points and that common right be done to all, rich as well as poor, without respect to persons.

> Again, Edward reassures the people that everyone is equal before the law. In a world where petty barons frequently raised armies to march against the king, this was calculated both to hold the barons in check and let the people know that the king was their friend. The lesson here is that it is more important to be a friend to the workforce than to middle management. Middle management can be replaced one at a time, at will, but if the workers are unhappy it can cause big trouble.

And because elections ought to be free, the King commandeth upon great forfeiture that no man by force of arms or by malice or menacing shall disturb any to make free elections.

> Free elections were practically unheard of in 13th-century England. This shows that Edward knew how to curry favour with his people; in effect, he gave them the right to make their own decisions on local affairs. Of course, if he did not like the results he always had the army.

The King hath granted unto his people that they shall have election of their sheriff in every shire, if they so desire.

> Much like the above, but here Edward is granting the election of Sheriff. This means that the people have been given the right to police themselves. Assuming that most people really do want order maintained, this should not be a dangerous step. The modern equivalent would be allowing the election of office or floor managers from among the ranks of the workers. Like Edward, if it doesn't work, the 'king' can always step in.

CORPORATE THEFT AND CRIME/CORPORATE PROTECTION

It is also provided that none, high or low born, by rank or kindred, affinity or alliance, or by any other occasion, shall ride in any park, fish in any pond, or come to eat or lodge in any house. . . against the will of the Lord, neither at the cost of the Lord, nor at his own.

> This is essentially a guard against trespass and confiscation of goods for personal use; it keeps low level management from using their power to abuse the workers. Abused workers will hate not only their oppressor but also their job and the company; malcontent workers simply will not perform.

No officer of ours, or of our heirs, shall take corn, leather or cattle, or any other goods, of any manner of person, without the good will and assent of the party to whom the goods belong.

> While nearly a duplicate of the law above, it was written nearly 30 years later. This may indicate that the barons did not listen the first time around and Edward felt the need to repeat himself. Sometimes, a point has to be made more than once for people to take it seriously.

Henceforth, none shall have writs of trespass brought before justices unless he swear by his faith that the goods taken away were worth 40 shillings at the least. And if he complain of a beating, he shall answer by his faith that his plaint is true, touching the wounds and maims.

> This is basically a matter of not bothering the grievance board with spurious or petty claims. Once indiscriminate complaining gets started it is nearly impossible to stop it: just look at the modern court system.

And it is to be known that if they to whom such trespass was done will sue for damages, the same shall be awarded and restored to double the amount claimed.

In the modern grievance system, be it civil court or an office arbitration, even the winner often loses because the time, stress and expense of the case has simply cost more than the matter is worth. Consequently, serious matters, particularly of an emotional nature, often go unresolved. Edward has provided for this by decreeing that the redress be double the amount claimed. Taken at face value, this doesn't seem unfair.

Forasmuch as merchants which heretofore have lent their goods to diverse persons, be greatly impoverished because there is no speedy law provided for them to have speedy recovery of their debts at the day of payment assigned. By reason hereof many merchants have withdrawn to come into this realm with their merchandises, to the damage of the merchants and of the whole realm. The King himself and by his council hath ordained and established that the merchant who is sure of his debt shall cause the debtor to come before the local mayor and his clerk for to acknowledge the debt and the day of payment. And the debt shall be entered into a roll by the hand of said clerk. Moreover, the said clerk shall make with his own hand a Bill Obligatory where unto the seal of the debtor shall be put along with the King's seal, which shall be provided for the purpose. And if the debtor doth not pay at the day to him limited, the creditor may come before the mayor and clerk with his Bill Obligatory. If it be found that the debt was acknowledged and the day of payment expired, the mayor shall cause the moveables of the debtor to be sold, as far as the debt doth amount, until the whole sum of the debt. . . shall be paid to the creditor.

This is a simple matter of contract law. In a world where it was nearly impossible to guarantee personal or property rights, Edward was doing his best to ensure that trade prospered. Then, like now, it only requires that the parties involved be wise enough never to enter into an agreement without writing it down and putting it on record.

Neither our justice in Ireland, nor any other of our officers there, by dint of their offices, shall take victuals or any other things of any person against his will, except in time of necessity, for the common profit of the realm; and then they shall [only] do it by the advice and assent of the greatest part of our council in those parts, and by a writ awarded out of our chancery in Ireland; and in such cases as We. . . do command by a writ awarded out of our chancery in England.

> Ireland was a peculiar case. It had been absorbed by England in an unfriendly takeover by Edward's army and the king wanted to do everything he could to reassure the Irish people that they would not be abused by his military governors. Rather than pass laws in favour of Irish merchants, he passed laws against abuses by his officials. The result is ultimately the same, but it is a clever manager who can make his underlings think he would take their side in opposition to middle management.

Moreover, that none of our justices, nor any of our other ministers, by dint of their office, shall arrest ships, nor other goods of strangers, or of our own people; but that all merchants and others may carry their corn and other victuals and merchandises, forth from our realm of Ireland. . . paying the customs due and used. And if any justice or other officer do the contrary in the things aforesaid, and be thereof [convicted], he shall satisfy the plaintiff double damages, and also shall be grievously punished by us.

> Much the same as above, but here the matter extends to non-interference. Essentially, it guarantees that the business of Ireland will not be raped and sold off for the profit of the new company managers.

It is provided that if a man leaves a rented property. . . even for a term of years, and the landlord is taken to court for colluding to legally deprive the lessor of the property, the lessor may recover the property by writ of covenant. The mayor and bailiffs shall make an inquest in the presence of the lessor and the landlord to discover whether the landlord had made his original plea on good right or by collusion or fraud to make the tenant lose his lease. If it be found by the inquest that the landlord moved his plea on good right, the judgement shall be given forthwith. But if it be found that he pleaded by fraud to put the tenant out of his lease, then the tenant shall enjoy the entirety of his term.

> This simple case of lease law has far-reaching implications. It ensures that those not fortunate enough to own their own property – and that was the vast majority in the middle ages – will not be abused by the more affluent merchant class. Protecting the rights of the workforce under your control is the first step in getting them on your side. Middle management may suffer as a result, but they were hired because they are efficient, not to be your friends.

CRIMINAL OFFENCES

It is provided and ordained that whereas the realm of England in diverse cases wherein the law failed to avoid grievous damages and innumerable faults. . . there is need to bring in new laws and certain provisions. These provisions, statutes and ordinances. . . shall from henceforth be straightly and inviolably observed by all the inhabitants of the realm. Whereas prelates, earls, barons and other of our realm that claim to have diverse liberties by which to examine and judge. . . shall use such manner of liberties after the form of writs here following.

> Here Edward admits that proper form is not being observed in administering his policies. To counter this problem the wise manager, like Edward, will devise a series of legal forms for local administrators to use in exercising their office. It is a simple matter of issuing a written job description laying out responsibilities and forms to ensure that they are carried out

accurately and responsibly.

For as much as there have been oftimes found in the country divisors of tales; whereby discord hath many times arisen between the King and his people, or great men of the realm; for the damage that hath, and may there from ensue, it is commanded that from henceforth none shall tell, or publish, any false news or tales whereby discord or slander may grow between the King and his people. And he that was the first author of such tales shall be taken and kept in prison until he is brought into court.

> In Edward's case this law was to prevent political dissension, but policies to stop gossip and the ever-present rumour mill from running rampant is never out of line. Of course, in the modern world, preventing rumours from spreading entails keeping the workforce apprised of what is actually going on, and this is always best done by the person ultimately in charge. People tend to stand by the boss's side if they feel they have been taken into his or her confidence.

Conspirators be they that do consider or bind themselves by oath, covenant or other alliance, that they shall aid and bear the other falsely and maliciously to indict or falsely to maintain pleas. . . and such as retain men in the countries with liveries to maintain their malicious enterprises, and this extends as well to the takers as to the givers. And stewards and bailiffs of Great Lords, which by their office or power undertake. . . to maintain quarrels or debates that concern other parties than such as touch the estates of their Lord or themselves.

> By issuing this definition of a conspirator Edward makes it clear what acts will be considered a direct threat to his power. He also makes clear how far the people can go without fearing reprisal. Making the rules clear is always good policy. As an historical point of interest, it was this law that was used to try and execute William Wallace in 1305.

QUEEN ELIZABETH I

Queen of England, born 1533, reigned 1558–1603

England's Elizabethan age is remembered today as an almost magical, glittering time, filled with music, magnificent clothes and great works of literature; but it did not begin that way. Elizabeth's grandfather, Henry VII, had seized the throne after a dynastic civil war that had raged across England for more than 30 years. Her father, Henry VIII, had transformed himself from a handsome, beloved young king to a tyrannical, grotesquely fat butcher who sent two of his wives and dozens of his friends to the block and ripped his kingdom apart by making war on the Catholic Church. Elizabeth's elder half-sister Mary had nearly destroyed the kingdom with religious pogroms: sending thousands of innocent people to the stake for their beliefs.

By the time Elizabeth came to the throne in 1558 she inherited a nation exhausted by strife, turmoil and cruelty. Personally highly strung and nervous, the 25-year old Elizabeth I quickly became a master at diplomatic procrastination. While her Ministers of State constantly urged action, the Queen consistently refused to be pushed into quick decisions. In 16th-century England, stepping with care was not only wise, it was essential; any other course of action could well have led the Queen and her kingdom to disaster.

Cautiously, Elizabeth set out to heal her land by the gentle, and dangerous, art of walking the political middle ground, which she called her 'golden mean'. She insisted that those who administered the law in her name be strong but fair; harsh measures were only to be used when the life of the kingdom, or of the Queen herself, was in peril. Above all, Elizabeth's most impressive political gift was making her mistrusting subjects believe that she loved them – each of them – as though they were her own family.

Throughout her 45-year reign Elizabeth constantly reiterated that it was from her subjects that her power flowed and therefore it was her duty to lead and protect them in the best way she knew how. For all her personal faults and vanities, Elizabeth was that rarest of human beings: a master propagandist and, at the same time, a truly enlightened leader.

Below is a short selection of her writings and speeches that indicate how, through kind words and humility, a person can establish a strong power base.

The passages have been edited and taken out of chronological order to fit conveniently under our modern-day topic headings.

DEALING WITH SUPERIORS

Was I not born in this realm? Were my parents born in any foreign country? Is not my kingdom here? Whom have I oppressed? Whom have I enriched to another's harm? What turmoil have I made in this Commonwealth that I should be suspected to have no regard to the same? As for my own part, I care not for death; for all men are mortal. And though I be a woman, yet I have as good a courage, answerable to my place, as ever my father had. I am your anointed Queen. I thank God that if I were turned out of the realm in my petticoat, I would be able to live anyplace in Christendom.

> Here, Elizabeth is defending herself against accusations by parliament that she was dragging her feet on important business.
>
> Her meaning is clear. When management has made no significant mistakes and has never ever harmed anyone under their control, the board of directors has no right to criticize them even if they do not move as fast as the board might like.

DEALING WITH YOUR
MIDDLE MANAGEMENT TEAM

Have a care over my people – they are *my* people. Every man oppresses them and despoils them without mercy. They cannot revenge their quarrels nor help themselves. See unto them, see unto them, for they are *my* charge.

This was Elizabeth's comment to a group of judges who came to pay their respects shortly after her coronation. Here the Queen shows that treating the general population fairly is imperative if top management is going to enjoy a peaceful reign; and it is the job of middle management (in this case the judges) to guarantee fair administration of the rules.

I must deal with nobles of diverse humours. . . and people who, although they make great demonstrations of love toward me, are nevertheless fickle and inconstant and I must fear everything.

Anyone in power is going to be surrounded by fawning 'yes' men who, despite what they say, are only looking for ways to advance themselves. Beware of these people, they do not care what happens to you.

I know no reason why any of my private answers to the realm should serve as a prologue to a subsidy book, neither yet do I understand why such audacity should be used to make, without my licence, an Act of my words.

A rare and important insight. The queen admonishes one of her ministers that her every word, particularly those said in private, should not be taken as an order. It is important that both middle management and the workers realize that the boss is also a private person. Only in those instances where something is intended as an order, or expressed as policy, should people base their actions on it. On the other hand, the boss is always in the public eye and he, or she, must be very careful of what they say or it may come back to haunt them.

This message we charge you to do as roundly and sharply as you can. . . for sure we are that you shall not express it with more vehemency than we mean and intend.

Removing doubt and confusion as to the specifics and importance of orders is essential if they are to be carried out in the manner in which they are intended.

DEALING WITH THE WORKFORCE

My loving people, We have been persuaded by some that are careful of our safety to take heed how we commit ourselves to armed multitudes, for fear of treachery. But I assure you, I do not desire to live to distrust my faithful and loving people. Let tyrants fear. I have always so behaved myself that, under God, I have placed my chiefest strength and safeguard in the loyal hearts and good will of my subjects, and therefore I come amongst you as you see at this time, not for my recreation and sport, but being resolved, in the midst and heart of the battle, to live or die amongst you all, to lay down for my God and for my kingdom and for my people, my honour and my blood, even in the dust. I know I have the body of a weak and feeble woman, but I have the heart and stomach of a king, and a King of England too, and think foul scorn that Spain or any Prince of Europe should dare to invade the borders of my realm, to which, rather than any dishonour shall grow by me, I myself will take up arms, I myself will be your general, judge and rewarder of every one of your virtues in the field. I know already for your forwardness you have deserved rewards and crowns, and we do assure you, in the word of a Prince, they shall be duly paid you. By your valour in the field, we shall shortly have a famous victory over these enemies of God, of my kingdom and of my people.

Before sending her soldiers and sailors out to face the Spanish Armada, Elizabeth rode among them and made this speech. It not only shows tremendous courage to have presented herself in a huge crowd where there could well have been assassins, but she makes a point of stating this in case its significance is lost on any of the men. Elizabeth says she is a 'weak and feeble woman' and states that she is willing to fight and die with her men. It is always good to get the workers' sympathy. Get them on your side first and then tell them you support their cause. Note that the Queen ends by promising the soldiers that they'll get paid whatever happens. Sympathy is good, standing together is good, but the workers are really there to get paid and they like to be sure the boss understands that fact. Like Elizabeth, learn to cover all the bases with style and grace.

It is a love of such a kind as has never been known or heard of in the memory of man. It is such a love as neither persuasion nor threats nor curses can destroy. Time has no power over it. Time, which eats away iron and wears away the rocks, cannot sever this love of yours.

The queen is addressing a crowd of her subjects on how touched she was with their devotion to her. Despite the fact that Elizabeth was constantly threatened by assassination plots cooked up by fanatics (particularly supporters of her cousin, Mary Queen of Scots), she knew that thanking the people for caring about her would strengthen their bonds of affection. This is like telling someone 'I know you would never lie to me', even when it is plain that they are. It puts them off balance and may actually shame them into behaving better in the future.

There is no jewel, be it of ever so rich a price, which I set before this jewel: I mean your love. For I do esteem it more than any treasure or riches; and though God has raised me high, yet this I count the glory of my crown that I have reigned with your love. My heart was never set upon any worldly goods, but only for my subjects' good. What you bestow upon me I will not hoard it up, but receive it to bestow upon you again. Yea, mine own properties I account as yours, to be expended for your good. There never will be a Queen who sits in my seat with more zeal for my country, care for my subjects and that will sooner with willingness venture her life for your good and safety than myself. And though you have had, and may have, many princes more mighty and wise sitting in this seat, yet you never had, nor shall have, any that will be more careful and loving.

> Here, the queen compares the love of her people to her great wealth and declares their loyalty the more important of the two. This is perfectly reasonable, because without popular support a general manager can lose their position. Company owners may not be in this position, but promising to use personal wealth for the benefit of the workers is a truly magnificent gesture of goodwill, even if it is no more than a gesture.

It shall not be lawful for any person to set up or use any craft or occupation within the realm of England or Wales, except he shall be brought up therein for seven years, at the least, as an apprentice, upon pain that every person willingly offending or doing the contrary shall forfeit for every default 40 shillings for every month of being unlawfully in business.

> This law was established to ensure that anyone practising a craft or trade had been properly schooled. Cleverly, the law not only ensures that the company, in this case the entire United Kingdom, meets the best possible standards, but also eliminates the threat of nepotism by ensuring that no one can circumvent the rules of apprenticeship. If your relatives want 'in' the business, they have to undergo training like everyone else. In a time when nearly every craftsman could take on apprentices, the soundest way to expand your business was to train your own future employees. It is a sound policy that virtually no one can argue with.

DEALING WITH THE COMPETITION

I am more afraid of making a fault in my Latin than of the Kings of Spain, France and Scotland, or of the whole house of Guise and all their confederates. I have the heart of a man, not a woman, and I am not afraid of anything.

> Elizabeth said this to the Spanish Ambassador when he brought news that Spain threatened to go to war with England. As a tiny, island nation England was vastly out-manned and out-gunned by Spain. It took great courage for Elizabeth to insist that she was more concerned with her Latin than with an invasion. The ploy did not work, however: Spain shortly launched its Armada against England. But there is no historical doubt that the Ambassador, and most of Spain, were cowed by this gutsy woman. Never let the competition see you sweat.

In such cases there is no middle course, we must lay aside clemency and adopt extreme measures. Yet, when the welfare of my state was concerned, I dared not indulge my own inclinations.

> As cool and self-assured as Elizabeth always appeared, she was in no doubt of the danger that constantly swirled around her. The above lines indicate that no matter how much you may wish to avoid conflict, be smart enough to know that sometimes there is no alternative. The difference between when to ponder and when to act is an instinct that all good managers have to develop.

If they shall not seem to you to confess plainly their knowledge, then we warrant you to cause them both, or either of them, to be brought to the rack and first to move them with fear thereof to deal plainly with their answers. Then, should the sight of the instrument not induce them to confess, you shall cause them to be put to the rack and to find the taste thereof till they shall deal more plainly or until you shall think fit.

Said to Sir Francis Walsingham, her spy-master, when a group of men were caught sending secret messages and money to aid Mary Queen of Scots in an attempt to overthrow Elizabeth. Obviously, a plot to overthrow the company calls for the most extreme reaction; still, spelling out the full consequences of someone's actions can often bring better results than extreme measures. Some plain speaking, rather than harsh action, can be a way out. Once a person has actually been fired, or disciplined, they have nothing left to lose and may not co-operate in clearing up a larger problem of which they may be only a small part.

You have in various ways and manners attempted to take my life and bring my kingdom to destruction by bloodshed. These treasons will be proved to you and all made manifest. It is my will that you answer the nobles and peers of the kingdom as if I were myself present. Act plainly without reserve and you will sooner be able to obtain favour of me.

Written in a letter to Mary Queen of Scots as she awaited trial for treason. Despite the continued attempts of Mary's supporters to overthrow Elizabeth, and even to have her assassinated, Elizabeth was still willing to grant Mary clemency if she would co-operate and admit her guilt. In part, this was a good political move: if Mary supplied the names of her co-conspirators their capture would help safeguard Elizabeth and undermine Mary. Sometimes, a little subterfuge can bring better, and safer, results than an all-out confrontation.

SECTION V

PHILOSOPHERS
AND SAGES

CONFUCIUS

Chinese philosopher and social critic, 551 BC–479 BC

While Confucius is undoubtedly the most recognizable name in the canon of classic Chinese literature, the content of his work remains largely unknown in the Western world.

Confucius, whose real name was K'ung-Fu-Tzu, was a teacher, philosopher, political critic and the most influential teacher in China's long history. Frustrated by his inability to break into the corrupt and notoriously nepotistic government of his native state of Lu, Confucius turned to the role of teacher. Gathering a group of disciples, he wandered the countryside expounding his views on the perfect society and how humanity had to change in order to achieve it.

His teachings were not, as is widely assumed, religious in nature. They were a code of moral ethics. The basis of this philosophy was concerned with achieving social change through ethical reform. Simply put, only when every individual had reformed himself, would society be transformed for the better.

What Confucius proposed was a society built with the family unit as the centre of its structure – in business, the boss represented the 'father figure', in politics it was the king. In each case, the 'father' was the unquestioned leader, and benevolent ruler, of the family unit. If this visionary society was to work, respect for the family structure must be paramount at all levels of society.

For the system to work, of course, the father figure, as well as everyone else, had to be enlightened enough to work for the common good. This enlightenment came in the form of what Confucius called 'jen'. Meaning both wisdom and spiritual balance, 'jen' was at the centre of Confucian philosophy. When a person achieves the state of 'jen', he or she would become what Confucius called a 'Superior Man'. For the purposes of clarity, we have substituted the more Western term 'wisdom' for the word jen in the following texts.

The writings and conversations of Confucius were eventually gathered into three texts, *The Analects*, *The Mean* and *The Great Learning*. Over time, the writings, and values of Confucius became the cornerstone of Chinese social literature and education, and remained so for more than 300 years.

Sadly, when Confucian concepts were put into practice by a society that had not reached a state of 'jen', the result was a damning, inflexible class system from which there was virtually no escape. But like the Bible, Talmud, Koran or other great works of wisdom, the fact that human beings fail to live up to the concept does not necessarily invalidate the message of the text.

The most famous of Confucius's works, *The Analects*, was compiled after his death by his students. It takes the form of conversations between Confucius, his students, friends and those who came to him seeking advice. It is from this book that the following selections have been gathered. Because of Confucius's concern with an individual's inner development, the majority of the epigrams selected here are also concerned with personal growth. For clarity, the text has been edited and rearranged under our modern-day topic headings.

DEALING WITH SUPERIORS

The reason that the Superior Man is easy to work for, but difficult to please, is because if you try to please him by devious means he will not be happy. And in his employment of people, he gives them work according to their ability. The Inferior Man is difficult to work for, but easy to please. Even if you have used devious means to please him he will still be happy. And in his employment of people, he tries to squeeze everything out of them that he can.

Beware of working for, or becoming, a person who expects results regardless of the consequences. The end does not always justify the means.

Be naturally courteous, be respectful in working for superiors and be sincere to people. Even the barbarian tribes cannot do without this.

There are few who have developed respect for their family and friends who will enjoy offending their superiors. Those who do not enjoy offending superiors are never trouble-makers.

People who are respectful outside the office will be respectful in the work environment.

If you use every single courtesy while serving your prince, the people will call you a sycophant.

An admonition against grovelling. Nobody likes, or trusts, a groveller.

It is better to value wisdom than passively to follow your teacher.

Claiming that you were 'only following orders' didn't work for the Nazis at Nuremburg and it doesn't work now.

In serving your prince, frequent remonstrance will lead to disgrace. With friends, frequent remonstrance will lead to separation.

If you criticize too often, or are too harsh in your criticism, people will resent you. Criticize only as necessary and then do it gently.

If you must oppose your leader, don't do it by deceit.

When you feel that you must criticize the boss, do it privately, and to their face. Never criticize, whine and complain behind their back. Word always gets around.

BECOMING AN EFFECTIVE MANAGER

If you would govern a state, you must pay strict attention to business, be true to your word, be economical in expenditure and love the people.

Be cautious and conservative in your thoughts and actions.

If you can practise these five things with all the people, you can be called a wise man. Courtesy, generosity, honesty, persistence and kindness. If you are courteous, you will not be disrespected; if you are generous, you will gain everything. If you are honest, people will rely on you. If you are persistent, you will get results. If you are kind, you can employ people.

What about 'fairness'? What you don't like done to yourself, don't do to others.

This is reminiscent of Jesus's admonishment to 'Do unto others as you would have them do unto you.'

These are the four characteristics of the Superior Man: In his private conduct he is courteous; in serving superiors he is respectful, in providing for the people he is kind; in dealing with the people he is just.

Like the item above, this has to do with treating other people the same way you expect to be treated.

The Superior Man is in harmony but does not follow the crowd. The Inferior Man follows the crowd, but is not in harmony.

The point here is that if you are truly wise, you can differentiate between following a trend because it is the right thing to do and following it just because it is popular.

Expect much from yourself and little from others and you will avoid incurring resentment.

Always expect more from yourself than you do from others and never ask someone else to do something that you would be ashamed to do yourself.

If you are strict with yourself, your mistakes will be few.

Self-discipline is one of the cornerstones of Confucian philosophy.

To make a mistake and not correct it: this is a real mistake.

Everyone makes mistakes, but trying to hide it, or deny it, is far worse than the mistake itself.

If you can correct yourself, what problem will you have in governing? If you can't correct yourself, how can you correct others?

You must have control over yourself before you can have control over other people.

When you see a good person, think of becoming like him or her. When you see someone not so good, reflect on your own weak points.

It probably won't help to condemn the faults of others, just see to it that you don't repeat their errors.

Each day I examine myself in three ways: in doing things for others, have I been loyal? In my interactions with friends, have I been trustworthy? Have I practised what I have preached?

If you don't have the official position, you can't plan the affairs of government. The Superior Man doesn't worry about those things which are outside of his control.

I don't worry about not having a good position; I worry about the means I use to gain position. I don't worry about being unknown; I seek to be known in the right way.

Almost anyone can make it to the top if they are clever. The important thing is to achieve success in the right way.

The Superior Man is aware of Righteousness, the Inferior Man is aware of advantage. If you do everything with a concern for your own advantage you will be resented by many people.

Like the previous quote, it is more important to do what is right than to advance yourself improperly, or at the expense of others.

When you see an opportunity for advantage, think of Righteousness. When you meet danger, leave it up to destiny. When someone reminds you of an old promise and it doesn't rattle you at all, you can be regarded as a 'perfected man'.

Speak enough to make the point, and then leave it at that.

Don't ramble on and don't talk a subject to death. Come to the point clearly and succinctly and then be quiet.

The Superior Man desires to be hesitant in speech, but sharp in action.

Think before you talk, and when you decide it is time to act don't hesitate.

The Superior Man is precise, but not rigid.

You should know precisely what you want people to do, but always be ready to listen to others' ideas and opinions.

Clever words disrupt virtue. Lack of patience in small matters leads to the disruption of great plans.

Don't be too clever for your own good and don't get so impatient that you take action before you know all the facts.

Don't be impatient, and don't look for small advantages. If you are impatient, you will not be thorough. If you look for small advantages, you will never accomplish anything great.

> As before, this advises you to pay attention to detail. It warns, however, that if you get bogged down in small, sneaky plans, the big opportunities will pass you by completely.

If you lack spiritual balance you can't handle long periods of difficulty or long periods of comfort.

SELECTING YOUR MIDDLE MANAGEMENT TEAM

To lead an army I would not select the kind of man who likes to wrestle with tigers or cross rivers on foot, or who would die without a second thought. It must be someone who approaches his business with caution, who likes to plan things well and see them to their completion.

> Don't employ people who make rash decisions, their recklessness could cause far more trouble than they are worth.

Observe a person's means of obtaining his goals. Observe his motives. How can a person conceal his character? I used to listen to what people said and expect them to act accordingly. Now I listen to what people say and watch what they do.

> No matter what a person says, if they are untrustworthy it will show in their behaviour. Don't just listen to what management candidates say, observe how they act.

People err according to their own level. It is by observing a person's mistakes that you can know his or her goodness.

> How someone deals with their mistakes, admitting them and trying to correct them or simply glossing them over, can tell you a lot about their character.

Someone may have profound theories – but is he a Superior Man? Or is he only superficially impressive?

> Learn to tell if a person is 'all talk' or if they really know what they are talking about.

The Superior Man does not promote a man because of his words, and does not disregard the words because of the man.

> Even someone whom you may not like can have good ideas. Don't disregard the ideas, but be cautious about promoting the person who made them.

Someone who is a clever speaker and maintains a 'too-smiley' face is seldom considered a person of good character.

> Beware of people who are too eager to please, they are probably hiding something.

The Superior Man is self-confident without being arrogant. The Inferior Man is arrogant and lacks self-confidence.

The Superior Man remains stable when in dire straits. The Inferior Man falls apart.

The Superior Man is humble in his speech but superb in his actions.

> A dynamic person does not need to brag. Their actions speak louder than their words ever could.

DEALING WITH YOUR MIDDLE MANAGEMENT TEAM

The prince employs his ministers with propriety; the ministers serve their prince with good faith.

If you don't demand unreasonable, or unethical, things from people they will treat you with respect.

The Superior Man does not let his Ministers feel resentment about not being utilized. Therefore, he doesn't dismiss anyone unless there is a really good reason, and he does not seek for all abilities in one man.

If you employ someone, always keep them busy, but use them to the best of their abilities. Don't expect them to do jobs for which they are not equipped.

When a person should be spoken to, and you don't speak to them, you lose them. When a person shouldn't be spoken to, and you speak to them, you waste your breath. The wise do not lose people, nor do they waste their breath.

Always keep your people 'in the loop', but don't bore them with endless, unnecessary information.

Inferior Men are hard to handle. If you get familiar with them, they lose their humility; if you are distant, they resent it.

If you are a good man and no one disagrees with you, it is fine. But if you are evil and no one disagrees with you, perhaps you could destroy the country with a single utterance.

Give your management people the confidence to disagree with you. It could keep you from making a dreadful mistake.

Only when good men have instructed the people for seven years may they take up arms. To lead untrained people into battle is the same as throwing them away.

Don't expect too much from your team too soon. Get comfortable with them and let them learn how you work and what you expect from them, before sending them out to do battle in your name.

DEALING WITH THE WORKFORCE

Govern by leading the people and working hard for them. Don't get discouraged.

When you have your own life straightened out, things will go well without having to give orders. But if your own life isn't straightened out, even if you give orders, no one will follow them.

People must have confidence in you before they will follow you.

If everybody hates something, you'd better look into it. If everybody loves something, you'd better look into it.

If you govern the people by the law alone and control them through punishment, they will avoid crime but will have no personal sense of shame. If you govern by propriety, the people will be respectful. If you govern them by means of virtue and control them with propriety, they will gain their own sense of shame and thus correct themselves.

It is far better to lead people by example than to drive them with a whip.

Approach your workers with dignity and they will be reverent. Be like a father and compassionate and they will be loyal. Promote the able and teach the incompetent, and they will work positively for you.

After the ruler has the trust of the people, they will toil for him. If he doesn't have their trust, they will regard him as oppressive. If they trust him, they will criticize him openly. If they don't trust him, they will slander him behind his back.

The boss is always going to be criticized. It is a lot better if your people are sufficiently comfortable with you to bring their grievances directly to you rather than complaining in private.

You might force people to act according to a certain principle, but you won't be able to force them to understand it.

It is not necessary for the workers to understand why you do everything that you do. What is important is that they trust you enough to follow you whether they understand your motives or not.

In teaching people, there must be no discrimination because of their social class.

This is just as true for race, religion and gender.

You can teach high level topics to those of above average ability, but you can't teach high level topics to those of less than average ability.

Don't expect more from people than they are capable of delivering. Just respect them for what they can do well.

When those in power lose their sense of justice, the people will scatter from them, and it will be a long time before they return. When you are aware of their suffering, then you should be sorrowful, never joyful.

Be fair with your people and they will trust you.

DEALING WITH BUSINESS ASSOCIATES

A friend asked Confucius:

'What do you think if all the people in town like you?'
'Not too good'

said Confucius.

'What if they all hate you?'

'Also not too good. It is better if the good people in town like you, and the evil ones hate you.'

There are three kinds of friendship that are beneficial and three kinds of friendship that are harmful. Friendship with the Righteous, friendship with the sincere and friendship with the learned are all beneficial. Friendship with the deceptive, friendship with the unprincipled and friendship with smooth talkers are harmful.

> Choose your friends and associates wisely.

The virtuous will certainly have something to say, but those who have something to say are not necessarily virtuous. The wise man is always brave, but the brave man is not necessarily possessed of wisdom.

> The trick, of course, is to learn to tell the difference!

Speak to your friends honestly, and skilfully show them the right path. If you cannot, then stop. Don't humiliate yourself.

> Advise people to the best of your ability, but they will only take your advice if they want to.

Base yourself in loyalty and trust. Don't be a companion with those who are not your moral equal. When you make a mistake, don't hesitate to correct it.

> Deceitful people may become rich and powerful and their success can make them a tempting ally, but be cautious in dealing with them. You will be seen as complicit in their dishonesty or, just as likely, they will turn on you.

Even the Superior Man has things that he hates. He hates those who advertise the faults of others. He hates those who abide in lowliness and slander the great. He hates those who are bold without propriety. He hates those who are convinced of their own perfection, and closed off to anything else.

There are three kinds of enjoyment that are beneficial and three kinds of enjoyment that are harmful. The enjoyment of cultivation in music and ritual, the enjoyment of speaking of the goodness of others and the enjoyment of being surrounded by friends of good character are all beneficial. The enjoyment of arrogance, the enjoyment of dissipation and the enjoyment of comfort are all harmful.

The Superior Man develops people's good points, not their bad points. The Inferior Man does the opposite.

If your paths are different, you cannot make plans together.

> No matter how close your friendship, or how close your business association with someone, if you are seeking essentially different goals it will be impossible for you to carry out long-term plans together.

WILLIAM SHAKESPEARE

English playwright and poet, 1564–1616

Shakespeare was undoubtedly one of history's most acute observers of human frailty. His insights into the human mind and soul are unparalleled. In 37 plays, written over a span of only 25 years, the Bard introduced us to heroes, villains, broken hearts, haunted spirits and mischievous fairies. While many of Shakespeare's historical plays rely more on fancy than fact, his characters (whether entirely fictional or not) are gems of insight. We have selected only two from among the hundreds of Shakespearean characters; neither of them are people you would want to deal with. But even the dull and the evil have lessons to teach in how – or how not – to conduct business.

The excerpts below are not edited or altered in any way. They are grouped under our contemporary headings.

HAMLET, PRINCE OF DENMARK

When Shakespeare created the character of Polonius, Lord Chamberlain to the King of Denmark, he brought to life a particular archetype that most of us have known at some point in our lives. Polonius is a giver of advice. . . lots of it. . . and the majority of what he says is both platitudinous and fatuous. He is also an incorrigible meddler in other people's business, and while he does not carry gossip, he is quick to pick it up.

Much of the advice Polonius gives to his son, Laertes, is sound; it is just phrased in such boring clichés that no one, neither his son nor the audience, can take it seriously. Polonius is often excused for being a crashing bore simply because he is old. The fact is, people don't change very much with age, they simply become more of whatever it is they were when they were young. Undoubtedly, Polonius was nearly as insufferable when he was young. The best thing to learn from this example is that Polonius serves as a perfect object lesson in how *not* to deal with other people.

Polonius dies on the end of a sword; it is a sad little moment that could have been avoided if he had not been standing behind a curtain eavesdropping on the conversation between Prince Hamlet and his mother, Queen Gertrude. This too serves as an object lesson.

DEALING WITH YOUR MIDDLE MANAGEMENT TEAM AND THE WORKFORCE

HAMLET ACT I, SCENE iii

Laertes is about to leave on a journey to France and his father, Polonius, is fumbling around, giving him 'good' advice as he leaves.

Polonius:
A double blessing is a double grace;
Occasion smiles on a second leave.
There, there, my blessing with thee!
And these few precepts in thy memory:

> Now, son, I'll give you my blessing, but take this advice to heart.

Give thy thoughts no tongue,
Nor any unproportion'd thought his act.

> Don't open your mouth or take any action unless you have thought it through first.

Be thou familiar, but by no means vulgar.

> Make new friends, but don't get too personal with people you don't know.

Those friends thou hast, and their adoption tried,
Grapple them to thy soul with hoops of steel.

> Always remember that old friends are the best.

But do not dull thy palm with entertainment
Of each new-hatched, unfledged comrade.

> Don't squander all your money running around with a bunch of people you aren't sure you can trust.

Beware of entrance to a quarrel, but being in,
Bear't that the opposed may beware of thee.

> Never pick a fight, but if you are forced into one, stand your ground.

Give every man thy ear, but few thy voice;

> Listen to what everybody has to say, but keep your own thoughts to yourself.

Take each man's censure, but reserve thy judgement.

> Don't be too easily offended and never offend anybody else.

Costly thy habit as thy purse can buy,
But not express'd in fancy; rich not gaudy
For the apparel oft proclaims the man.

> Always dress well. Be fashionable but don't buy trashy looking clothes just
> because they are popular. People judge you by the way you dress.

And they in France of the best rank and station
Are most select and generous, chief in that.

> The French are the most stylish people in the world. . . for heaven's sake,
> don't dress like a bum in front of the French.

Neither a borrower nor a lender be;
For loan oft loses both itself and friend.

> Don't lend or borrow money, it is a good way to lose both your cash and
> your friends.

This above all: to thine own self be true,
And it must follow as the night follows day,
Thou canst not be false to any man.

> Most importantly, be a good boy. As long as you are honest with yourself,
> you will be honest with other people.

At this point, Laertes finally escapes.

As we said before, the advice is so poorly given it would be hard for
anyone to take seriously. Pity, too; most of the advice still holds true
after more than 400 years.

THE MERCHANT OF VENICE

Throughout the middle ages and renaissance, Christians were prohibited by the Church from lending money at a profit because to do so was defined as usury, which was considered by the Church to be a sin. Since people always need to borrow money, be it a merchant looking to expand their business or a king who needs to finance a war, and with virtually no one willing to lend money interest free, the economic gap had to be filled by someone. The 'someone' was the Jewish community; as non-Christians they were not constrained by Church law and as a community of merchants they often had spare cash.

Inevitably, resentment arose between Christians and Jews. When a Christian needed money he had no other recourse than to turn to the money lenders and pay interest, which he believed was opposed to the teachings of the Church. The Jews were equally resentful because they were reviled for filling a necessary niche in the economic community.

In Shakespeare's play, *The Merchant of Venice*, the merchant in question, Antonio, is approached by his friend, Bassanio, for a loan to finance, of all things, a love affair. All of Antonio's money is invested in several shiploads of goods which have not arrived in Venice. Nevertheless, he agrees to help Bassanio by borrowing money from Shylock, a Jewish money-lender. Shylock has no love for Antonio, who is a known anti-Semite, renown for making interest-free loans to his friends and so, perceives him as cutting into one of the few areas where Jews are legally allowed to prosper.

Shylock agrees to the loan, but insists that if Antonio cannot pay the capital and interest on the appointed day, he is to forfeit a pound of flesh cut from his body. It seems overly harsh, but given the animosity between the Christian and Jewish communities at the time, it is hardly surprising that Shylock wanted to make an example of Antonio. Foolishly, the arrogant Antonio agrees to the terms. Obviously, Antonio is unable to repay the loan so Shylock takes him to court and demands that he submit to the grizzly payment.

Whatever else it may be, *The Merchant of Venice* is a story of two men who foolishly lock themselves into a mutually disagreeable contract; here alone is an important management lesson. One of the men is too arrogant to realise that this was a stupid deal and the other is too stubborn to accept a mutually amenable compromise when it is offered to him.

DEALING WITH BUSINESS ASSOCIATES

THE MERCHANT OF VENICE ACT I, SCENE iii

We take up the story at the point where Bassanio, representing Antonio, approaches Shylock.

Shylock: Three thousand ducats; well.

Bassanio: Ay, sir, for three months.

Shy: For three months; well.

Bass: For the which, as I told you, Antonio shall be bound.

Shy: Antonio shall be bound; well.

Bass: May you stead me? Will you pleasure me? Shall I know your answer?

Shy: Three thousand ducats for three months and Antonio shall be bound.

Bass: Your answer to that?

Shy: Antonio is a good man.

Bass: Have you heard any imputation to the contrary?

Shy: Oh, no, no, no, no: my meaning, in saying he is a good man, is to have you understand me that he is sufficient. Yet his means are in supposition: he hath an argosy bound to Tripolis, another to the Indies; I understand, moreover, upon the Rialto, he hath a third at Mexico, a fourth for England, and other ventures he hath, squandered abroad. But ships are but boards, sailors but men: there be land rats and water rats, water thieves and land thieves, I mean pirates, and then there is the peril of waters, winds and rocks. The man is, notwithstanding, sufficient. Three thousand ducats; I think I may take his bond.

Bass: Be assured you may.

Shy: I will be assured I may; and that I may be assured, I will bethink me. May I speak with Antonio?. . .

For reasons unknown, Antonio allows Bassanio to approach Shylock instead of doing it himself. When a person has important business at hand they should attend to it themselves or appoint an official representative, not send a friend.

Throughout most of this exchange, Shylock repeats everything that Bassanio tells him. He is obviously buying time to consider the request. As the conversation develops we can tell that Shylock is ruminating on the character of Antonio, whom he obviously knows and just as obviously mistrusts. While business is business and personal relationships should not enter into it, it is a foolish person who allows themselves to enter into a business deal with someone whom they mistrust or, worse yet, hate. Long-standing mistrust will inevitably sour even the most lucrative business opportunity.

Shortly after this exchange Antonio enters the scene.

Bass: This is Signior Antonio.

Shy: [Aside, to the audience] How like a fawning publican he looks?
I hate him for he is a Christian.
But more for that in low simplicity
He lends out money gratis and brings down
The rate of usury here with us in Venice.
If I can catch him once upon the hip,
I will feed the ancient grudge I bear him.
He hates our sacred nation, and he rails,
Even there where merchants most do congregate,
On me, my bargains and my well-won thrift,
Which he calls interest. Cursed be my tribe
If I will forgive him. . .

> So now we know why Shylock hates Antonio, the question is, why would
> Antonio be so stupid as to approach Shylock? At this point, their mutual
> dislike has not come out into the open, but as in all business dealings with
> an enemy, it is only a matter of time.

Antonio: Shylock, although I neither lend nor borrow
By taking nor giving of excess,
Yet, to supply the ripe wants of my friend,
I'll break a custom. Is he yet possessed
How much ye would?

Shy: Ay, ay, three thousand ducats.

Ant: And for three months.

168

Shy: I had forgot; three months, you told me so.
Well then, your bond; and let me see; but hear you;
Methought you said you neither lend nor borrow
Upon advantage.

> Having made the first mistake of dealing with someone whom he has pub-
> licly insulted, Antonio compounds the situation by being caught in an obvi-
> ous and transparent lie – Shylock already knows Antonio loans money.
> Now Antonio insists that he does not borrow, when that is obviously what
> the conversation is all about. In business dealings it is an absolute neces-
> sity to keep some important information to yourself, but when there are
> salient facts, even personal ones, of which all parties are aware, the wise
> man puts them on the table from the outset to defuse a possibly damag-
> ing situation.

Ant: I do never use it.

Shy: Three thousand ducats; tis a good round sum.
Three months from twelve; then let me see; the rate –

Ant: Well, Shylock, shall we be beholding to you?

Shy: Signior Antonio, many a time and oft
In the Rialto you have [be]rated me
About my moneys and my usury:
Still have I born it with a patient shrug,
For sufferance is the badge of all our tribe.
You call me misbeliever, cut-throat dog,
And spit upon my Jewish gaberdine,
And all for use of that which is mine own.
Well then, it now appears you need my help:
Go to, then; you come to me, and you say,

'Shylock, we would have moneys'. . .
Shall I bend low, in a bondsman's key,
With bated breath and whispering humbleness,
Say this:
'Fair sir, you spit on me on Wednesday last:
You spurned me on such a day: another time
You called me dog: and for these courtesies
I'll lend you this much moneys?'

> Shylock has now made it obvious that he does not want to deal with
> Antonio. When a situation like this occurs, it doesn't take a rocket scien-
> tist to know that things are only going to get worse and the negotiations
> should be brought to a halt before one, if not both, parties get them-
> selves into a position from which there is no viable way out. Antonio is
> obviously not a smart man. In the following exchange, notice how he con-
> tinues to goad Shylock.

Ant: I am as like to call thee so again,
To spit on thee again, to spurn thee too.
If thou wilt lend this money, lend it not
As to thy friends. . .
But lend it rather to thine enemy,
Who, if he break, thou mayst with better face
Exact the penalty. . .

Shy: This kindness will I show.
Go with me to a notary, seal me there
Your single bond; and, in merry sport,
If you repay me not on such a day,
In such a place, such a sum or sums as are
Expressed in the condition, let the forfeit
Be nominated for an equal pound

Of your fair flesh, to be cut off and taken
In what part of your body pleaseth me.

Ant: Content, in faith; I'll seal to such a bond,
And say there is much kindness in the Jew...
I will not forfeit it;
Within these two months, that's a month before
This bond expires, I do expect return
Of thrice three times the value of this bond.

> Shylock has done Antonio the favour of making the terms of the loan so
> ridiculously unpalatable that no one in their right mind would accept.
> Amazingly, Antonio does. This goes way beyond the ability to recognize
> the signs of a business deal going bad; anyone who puts themselves in
> this kind of a situation deserves what they get. Always make business deci-
> sions with cold, detached common sense, never with pride and ego. There
> are always situations beyond our ability to control; try to allow yourself
> room to manoeuvre if one of them strikes.

ACT IV, SCENE i

We pick up the story in court. Shylock has brought Antonio before the
Duke to exact the terms of the contract. From somewhere, Bassanio
has come up with six thousand ducats, which he offers Shylock if he
will release Antonio from the terms of the contract.

Shy: If every ducat in six thousand ducats
Were in six parts and every part a ducat,
I would not draw them; I would have my blood.

Duke: How shalt thou hope for mercy, rendering none?

Shy: What judgement shall I dread, doing
  no wrong?
You have among you purchased many a slave,
Which, like your asses and your dogs and mules,
You use in abject and in slavish parts,
Because you bought them: shall I say to you,
Let them be free, marry them to your heirs?
Why sweat they under your burdens? Let their beds
Be made as soft as yours, and let their palates
Be seasoned with such viands? You will answer
'The slaves are ours': so do I answer you:
The pound of flesh, which I demand of him,
Is dearly bought; tis mine and I will have it.

> Here, Shylock has reduced himself to the level of pure vengeance. If pre-
> sented with an opportunity to have a significant economic victory or a des-
> picable moral one, a wise businessman takes the money and leaves his
> dubious moral superiority at home. Business is not about making a point,
> nor should it be personal: it is about helping your business succeed. This
> is something Shylock obviously knows, but he has allowed his hatred of
> Antonio to get the better of his business sense; an easy mistake to make
> in the heat of passion. The best way to avoid this kind of disaster is never
> to allow yourself to get caught in this type of situation in the first place.
> Both of these men had the opportunity to get out of this mess. Shylock
> could have refused to make the loan. Antonio, even if he was stupid
> enough to have approached someone he hated, should have backed down
> when the ridiculous terms of default were presented to him.

Shakespeare being Shakespeare, Shylock is eventually out-manoeuvred
and loses not only the loan, his profit and interest, but half his personal fortune as well. Partly, this is because much of 16th-century
England was anti-Semitic and Shakespeare was not only a victim of this,
but he was also undoubtedly pandering to his audience's prejudices.

Of course, there are also the convolutions present in all Shakespearian love stories: in this case the destruction of Shylock allows the love between the none-too-clever Bassanio and his lady to flourish. It is a silly story, but the lessons in how *not* to conduct business should be far more evident to any astute person today than they were to the play-going audience of 1605, when this work was first performed.

BENJAMIN FRANKLIN

American diplomat and statesman, 1706–1790

Benjamin Franklin was a most unlikely revolutionary. Best known as a diplomat, Franklin also established the United States postal system and what was probably the world's first mail-order business, dealing in scientific books and literature. He never sought power or personal political gain and was more interested in finding common ground and reaching amicable reconciliation than in rattling sabres. A man of letters, with broad-ranging sympathies, his staunch Quaker upbringing, if not his rational approach to life, would have prohibited his taking up arms against his government.

With the sympathetic ear of British Prime Minister, William Pitt, Franklin tried desperately to find a way to prevent armed conflict between the American colonies and the British Empire; partly because he hated violence and partly because he saw no chance of America winning the conflict. Had it not been for Britain's simultaneous involvement in a war with France, history would probably have proven him right.

So respected was Franklin, that despite his advanced age he was called upon to act as minister to France – ostensibly to raise aid money – during the Revolutionary War. His reputation as a great thinker preceded him. While in Paris, he was sought out and courted by the great luminaries of French literary and political society. Voltaire reputedly said of him: 'He has the finest mind I have ever met.'

Franklin's personal morality made him disassociate himself from anyone he considered to be self-serving or corrupt. His dislike for George Washington, although played down by history, was legendary in Revolutionary America. For nearly 20 years Franklin refused even to be in the same room with Washington, insisting that he had only voted for him as head of the Continental Army because 'when mounted on the back of his huge, bay coloured horse he made a fine target for the lobster backs' (referring to the red-coated British soldiers).

While his fellow countrymen Sam Adams and Thomas Paine were churning out inflammatory pamphlets against the British, Franklin, never prone to rash actions, contented himself with gently poking fun at British policies which he found both incomprehensibly stiff-necked and illogical. Yet he did so without ever mentioning either Great Britain or the American colonies by name. Franklin's only political commentary, *Rules for Reducing a Great Empire to a Small One*, is reprinted here in an edited and abbreviated form. The order of the text remains unaltered, although it appears under our modern-day heading. Bear in mind that this is satire, so the advice Franklin gives will do no more than ensure disaster for the 'Great Empire' in question.

FROM *RULES FOR REDUCING A GREAT EMPIRE TO A SMALL ONE*

MANAGING A SUBSIDIARY COMPANY

I. A great empire, like a great cake, is most prone to crumble at the edges. Turn your attention, therefore, first to your remotest provinces so, that as you get rid of them, the next may follow in order.

Don't ignore those parts of your business most removed from your daily routine. Deterioration often starts when we fall into an 'out of sight, out of mind' mentality.

II. Take special care the provinces never enjoy the same common rights and privileges in commerce as the mother country and that they are governed by severer laws, all enacted without allowing them to share in the choice of legislators.

> Always deal equally with those under your control. No business can succeed when one set of rules or standards is applied to one group and a different one to another.

III. Those remote provinces that have been acquired, purchased or conquered at the sole expense of the settlers of their ancestors, without the aid of the mother country, but forget their hard won strength and treat them as if they had done you some injury and contrive to punish them for it.

> If you take over a business, or a department, always give credit to those who came before you, whether they were in positions of management or were simply the workers who kept the place running prior to your arrival or involvement.

IV. However peacefully your colonies have submitted to your government. . . suppose that they are always inclined to revolt and treat them accordingly. By this means you may, in time, convert your suspicions into realities.

> Don't treat people in your charge like the enemy, treat them as though you need them, because the fact is, you do.

V. Remote provinces must have governors and judges. . . and much of the strength of the government depends on the people's opinion of these men. If you send them wise and good men for governors. . . they will think their king wise and good. You are therefore to be careful to find for judges and governors. . . prodigals. . . who will probably be rapacious and provoke the people. . . If they should be ignorant, wrong-headed and insolent, so much the better.

> This is a subject that comes up again and again in this book. Your people will always judge you by your representatives – middle management. If middle management is good and fair, the workers will think the same of you; if they are harsh, your people will hate you by association, if for no other reason.

VI. To confirm the colonists' impressions. . . when the injured come to the capitol with complaints of mal-administration, oppression or injustice, punish them with long delays, enormous expense and final judgement in favour of the oppressor. . . thence, the people well may become more disaffected and, at length, desperate.

> Don't compound problems by trying to deal with them through mindless bureaucracy – it will only make things worse.

VII. When such governors have crammed their coffers and made themselves so odious to the people that they can no longer remain among them with safety. . . reward them with pensions. This will contribute to encourage new governors in the same practice and make the supreme government detestable.

> Dealing with incompetent middle managers, or employees, by transferring them to other departments does not solve anything. It just moves the problem around. Remember, if you transfer your problems to another department, other departments will do the same to you. The best course of action: fire them. Now!

VIII. Reflect that a penny taken from them by your power is more honourable to you than a pound presented by their benevolence, so despise their voluntary grants and resolve to harass them with novel taxes. Remember to make your tax more grievous by public declarations importing that your power of taxing them has no limits. This will weaken every idea of security and convince them that they have nothing to call their own.

> A sense of self-worth and a feeling of personal security is absolutely essential to maintain a functional atmosphere at home or at work. If people are denied these basic emotional supports, they will not respect themselves or their bosses and they will not co-operate with the company or among themselves.

IX. Never regard the heavy burden those people already undergo. Forget the restraint you lay on their trade for your own benefit and the advantage a monopoly of this trade gives your merchants. Think nothing of the wealth those merchants and your manufacturers acquire by the colony's commerce.

> Management too often assumes that the workforce does not understand the problems of being in charge. They probably don't, but this because they have problems of their own: try to take this into account when making demands on them. Remember that without the respect and goodwill of the workforce, management would have nothing to manage. Try to work together for the economic benefit of the business. Prosperity solves a lot of personal problems.

X. Perplex their commerce with infinite regulations, impossible to be remembered and observed. Ordain seizures of their property for every failure. . . and let there be a formal declaration. . . that opposition to your edicts is treason and that persons suspected of treason. . . may be seized. . . for trial. This will. . . convince them that they are. . . under a power. . . which cannot only kill their bodies but damn their souls.

> Like item VI above, the proliferation of mindless bureaucracy doesn't solve problems, it *is* a problem.

XI. To make your taxes more odious and more likely to procure resistance, send. . . a board of officers to superintend the collection, composed of the most indiscreet, ill-bred and insolent you can find. . . If any revenue officers are suspected of the least tenderness for the people, discard them.

> Boards of review, efficiency experts and committees set up to 'streamline' businesses all too often behave like storm troopers. Even if their job involves eliminating jobs, they need not carry it out like an inquisition: if they do, it will reflect on those who called them in.

XII. Another way to make your tax odious is to misapply the produce of it. If it was originally appropriated for the defence of the provinces . . . then apply none of it to that defence. . . This will make them pay it more unwillingly and be more apt to quarrel with those that collect it. . . and shall contribute to your own purpose of making them weary of your government.

> This point is highly relevant to some of the pension plan scandals of the 1970s and 1980s. A company that robs its employees is, inevitably, robbing itself.

XIII. If the people of any province have been accustomed to support their own governors and judges. . . you are to apprehend such governors and judges as may be influenced to treat the people kindly and do them justice. . . Thus, the people may no longer hope for any kindness from their governors or justice from their judges.

> Again, like Machiavelli, Franklin is urging for responsible middle management. If you have efficient and well-liked middle management people in place, don't move them. They keep your people happy. If they are moved to another department they have to rebuild that trust with a new group and whoever replaces them may well be resented.

XIV. If the parliaments of your provinces should dare to claim rights, or complain of your administration, order them to be harassed and dissolved. If the same men are continually returned by new elections, adjourn their meetings. This. . . is your prerogative and an excellent one. . . to promote discontent among the people, diminish their respect and increase their disaffection.

> Do not undermine the authority of workers' representatives and collective bargaining boards. If you do, you will be seen as a dictator.

XV. If you are told of discontent in your colonies, never believe they are general or that you have given any occasion for them. Therefore, do not think of applying any remedy or of changing any offensive measure. Redress no grievance, lest they should be encouraged to demand redress of some other grievance. Grant no request that is just and reasonable, lest they should make another. . . Suppose all their complaints to be invented and promoted by a few factious demagogues who, if you could catch and hang, all would be quiet.

> While spies are generally bad things, it is absolutely necessary to find out what the workers think about management. If possible, go, like Shakespeare's Henry V, among them in disguise and talk to them. If that is not possible (and it probably isn't) then find out some other way, because the fact is, 'workers' will almost never tell management what they are thinking: at least not until it is too late.

XVI. If you see rival nations rejoicing at the prospect of your disunion with your provinces and endeavouring to promote it, let not that alarm or offend you. Why should you, since you all mean the same thing?

> If things have become so bad that you hear from the competition that your company is having worker/management problems, you are on the edge of disaster.

XVII. Lastly, invest the general of your army in the provinces with great and unconstitutional powers and free him from the control of even your own civil governors. And who knows but he may take it into his head to set up for himself. If he should, take my word for it, the provinces will immediately join him – and you will get rid of the trouble of governing them once and forever.

> Never allow middle management, or those who manage in your absence, to become loose cannons. They will undermine your authority and the workers' respect for you quicker than anything on earth.

ELBERT HUBBARD

—— ა ——

American businessman and social philosopher, 1856–1915

Elbert Hubbard was something of a late 19th-century phenomenon. Having made a sizeable fortune selling soap for a company in which he owned a part interest, Hubbard is credited with being one of the fathers of modern advertising. In his early forties he sold his interest in the company and set up the Roycroft press in East Aurora, New York, which he modelled on William Morris's Kelmscott Press in England. Roycroft expanded into a community of artists and craftsmen whose designs Hubbard expounded in two periodicals, *The Philistine* and *The Fra*. Filling the pages of both magazines with his own stories and epigrams, Hubbard became one of the best-known American writers of the period.

In a world of staid, Victorian gentlemen Hubbard was something of an anomaly. Turning his back on top hats and tails, Hubbard preferred gigantic, fluffy bow ties and long hair, taking on the air of a Victorian hippie. Politically he was an odd combination of the traditional,

Protestant work ethic and a radically progressive social consciousness.

His 1899 piece, *A Message to Garcia*, catapulted him to the status of world celebrity. Tens of thousands of copies were distributed around the world to government employees, the soldiers of half a dozen nations and employees of various companies including the HJ Heinz Corporation (see our chapter on Henry J Heinz, p.69). On a personal peace mission to Europe during the early years of World War I, Hubbard and his wife died when the *Lusitania*, on which they were travelling, was sunk by a German submarine in 1915.

All of Hubbard's pieces that appear below are printed in their entirety. Again, they are grouped under our (single) topic heading.

DEALING WITH SUPERIORS

This little proverb is one of many that Hubbard wrote for inclusion in one of his periodicals.

If you work for a man, in heaven's name work for him; speak well of him and stand by the institution he represents. Remember, an ounce of loyalty is worth a pound of cleverness. If you must growl, condemn and eternally find fault, resign your position and when you are on the outside, damn to your heart's content – but as long as you are part of the institution do not condemn it. If you do, the first high wind that comes along will blow you away, and probably you will never know why.

The following piece, *A Message to Garcia*, was, until recent years, the most popular and frequently printed piece of management advice ever published.

It concerns an episode that happened during the Spanish–American War (April-December 1898). A few months after the war, the incident was supposedly brought to Hubbard's attention by his son. The tale so inspired Hubbard that he dashed off the following piece in a single hour, following his evening meal on Washington's birthday (22 February) 1899.

Printed in the same month's edition of *The Philistine*, the piece excited so much attention that it almost immediately appeared in major newspapers and periodicals across the country. Hubbard himself published it as a six-page booklet. Within three years it achieved global distribution including publications specifically for the Russian and Japanese military, the US Navy and railroad workers on three continents.

Hopefully its appearance here will help revive its popularity. Do not mistake the exclusively masculine references as sexist. Remember, Hubbard was writing in 1899 when universities and places of business were almost exclusively male preserves.

The piece appears in its entirety.

A MESSAGE TO GARCIA

In all this Cuban business there is one man who stands out on the horizon of my memory like Mars at perihelion. When war broke out between Spain and the United States, it was very necessary to communicate quickly with the leader of the Insurgents; Garcia was somewhere in the mountainous vastness of Cuba – no one knew where. No mail or telegraph could reach him. The President must secure his co-operation, and quickly.

What to do! Someone said to the President, 'There's a fellow by the name of Rowan will find Garcia for you, if anybody can.'

Rowan was sent for and given a letter to be delivered to Garcia. How 'the fellow by the name of Rowan' took the letter, sealed it up in an oil-skin pouch, strapped it over his heart, in four days landed by night off the coast of Cuba from an open boat, disappeared into the jungle, and in three weeks came out on the other side of the island, having traversed a hostile country on foot, and having delivered his letter to Garcia, are things I have no special desire now to tell in detail.

The point I wish to make is this: [President William] McKinley gave Rowan a letter to be delivered to Garcia; Rowan took the letter and did not ask, 'Where is he at?' By the Eternal! There is a man whose form should be cast in deathless bronze and the statue placed in every college in the land. It is not book-learning young men need, nor instruction about this or that, but a stiffening of the vertebrae which will cause them to be loyal to a trust, to act promptly, concentrate their energies; to do the thing – 'carry a message to Garcia!'

General Garcia is dead now, but there are other Garcias. No man who has endeavoured to carry out an enterprise where many hands were needed, but has been well-nigh appalled at times by the imbecility of the average man – the inability or unwillingness to concentrate on a thing and do it. Slipshod assistance, foolish inattention, dowdy indifference and half-hearted work seem the rule; and no man succeeds, unless by hook or crook, or threat, he forces or bribes other men to assist him; or mayhap, God in His goodness performs a miracle and sends him an Angel of Light for an assistant. You, reader, put this matter to a test: You are sitting now in your office – six clerks are within your call. Summon any one and make this request: 'Please look in the encyclopedia and make a brief memorandum for me concerning the life of Correggio.'
Will the clerk quietly say 'Yes sir' and go do the task?

On your life, he will not. He will look at you out of a fishy eye, and ask one or more of the following questions:

'Who was he?'

'Which encyclopedia?'

'Where is the encyclopedia?'

'Was I hired for that?'

'Don't you mean Bismarck?'

'What's the matter with Charlie doing it?'

'Is he dead?'

'Is there any hurry?'

'Shan't I bring you the book and let you look it up yourself?'

'What do you want to know for?'

And I will lay you ten to one that after you have answered the questions, and explained how to find the information, and why you want it, the clerk will go off and get one of the other clerks to help him find Garcia – and then come back and tell you there is no such man. Of course, I may lose my bet, but according to the Law of Averages, I will not.

Now, if you are wise you will not bother to explain to your 'assistant' that Correggio is indexed under the C's, not in the K's, but you will smile sweetly and say 'Never mind' and go look it up yourself.

And this incapacity for independent action, this moral stupidity, this infirmity of the will, this unwillingness cheerfully to catch hold and lift, are the things that put pure socialism so far into the future. If men will not act for themselves, what will they do when the benefit of their effort is for all? A first mate with knotted club seems necessary; and the dread of getting 'the bounce' Saturday night holds many a worker in his place.

Advertise for a stenographer, and nine out of ten who apply can neither spell nor punctuate – and do not think it necessary to. Can such a one carry a letter to Garcia?

'You see that bookkeeper?' said the foreman to me in a large factory.

'Yes, what about him?'

'Well, he's a fine accountant, but if I'd send him to town on an errand, he might accomplish the errand all right, and, on the other hand, might stop at four saloons on the way, and when he got to Main Street would forget what he had been sent for.' Can such a man be entrusted to carry a message to Garcia?

We have recently been hearing much maudlin sympathy expressed for the 'down-trodden denizen of the sweat shop' and the 'homeless wanderer searching for honest employment', and with it often go many hard words for the men in power.

Nothing is said about the employer who grows old before his time in a vain attempt to get frowsy ne'er-do-wells to do intelligent work; and his long patient striving with 'help' that does nothing but loaf when his back is turned. In every store and factory there is a constant weeding-out process going on. The employer is constantly sending away 'help' that have shown their incapacity to further the interests of the business, and others are being taken on. No matter how good times are, this sorting continues, only if times are hard and work is scarce this sorting is done finer – but out and forever out, the incompetent and unworthy go. It is the survival of the fittest. Self-interest prompts every employer to keep the best – those who can carry a message to Garcia.

I know one man of really brilliant parts who has not the ability to manage a business of his own, and yet who is absolutely worthless to anyone else because he carries with him constantly the insane suspicion that his employer is oppressing, or intending to oppress, him. He cannot give orders, and he will not receive them. Should a message be given him to take to Garcia, his answer would probably be 'Take it yourself.'

Tonight this man walks the streets looking for work, the wind whistling through his threadbare coat. No one who knows him dare employ him, for he is a regular firebrand of discontent. He is impervious to reason, and the only thing that can impress him is the toe of a thick-soled No.9 boot.

Of course, I know that one so morally deformed is no less to be pitied than a physical cripple; but in your pitying, let us drop a tear, too, for the men who are striving to carry on a great enterprise, whose working hours are not limited by the whistle, and whose hair is fast turning white through the struggle to hold the line in dowdy indifference, slipshod imbecility and the heartless ingratitude which, but for their enterprise, would be both hungry and homeless.

Have I put the matter too strongly? Possibly I have; but when all the world has gone a-slumming I wish to speak a word of sympathy for the man who succeeds – the man who, against great odds, has directed the efforts of others and, having succeeded, finds there's nothing in it: nothing but bare board and clothes.

I have carried a dinner-pail and worked for a day's wages, and I have also been an employer of labour, and I know there is something to be said on both sides. There is no excellence, *per se*, in poverty; rags are no recommendation; and all employers are not rapacious and high-handed, any more than all poor men are virtuous.

My heart goes out to the man who does his work when the 'boss' is away, as well as when he is home. And the man who, when given a letter for Garcia, quietly takes the missive without asking any idiotic questions and with no lurking intention of chucking it into the nearest sewer or of doing aught else but deliver it, never gets 'laid off' nor has to go on strike for higher wages. Civilization is one long anxious search for just such individuals. Anything such a man asks will be granted; his kind is so rare that no employer can afford to let him go. He is wanted in every city, town and village – in every office, shop, store and factory. The world cries out for such; he is needed, and needed badly – the man who can carry a message to Garcia.

> Despite the slightly long-winded Victorian prose, and the obvious fact that Hubbard is too personally involved in his subject, the importance of what is being said here is obvious. In the modern, hi-tech world we have come to think that lax and sloppy work habits are something new – or at least date from no earlier than the 1960s: obviously this is not the case. But now, as then, the importance of being what is known as a 'self-starter' cannot be over-stated.
>
> No matter how high we are on the totem pole, we are all answerable to someone: our boss, our clients and, yes, even our employees. If management does not set an example of hard work and diligence how can it expect those beneath it to exercise the same qualities? At the very least, if the boss is lax he deprives himself of any moral ground for demanding those in his charge to put forth their best efforts. If you work hard, only a few people will ever notice, but if you are lazy, everyone will notice.

MAXIMS AND CLEVER SAYINGS

Hubbard filled the pages of his magazines with clever, 'folksy' epigrams, virtually all of which he devised himself. Some of them were humorous and some, by modern standards, maudlinly sentimental. But many gave sound advice on attitudes towards work. A few of the best appear below. As they are self-explanatory, no comment is offered.

If you want work done well, select a busy man; the other kind has no time.

The best preparation for good work tomorrow is to do good work today.

Thoroughness characterizes all successful men. Genius is the art of taking infinite pains. All great achievement has been characterized by extreme care, infinite, painstaking, even to the minutest detail.

Do not expect gratitude, but when you find it, be grateful.

To avoid criticism: Do nothing, say nothing, be nothing!

It is a fine thing to have ability, but the ability to discover ability in others is the true test.

People who never do more than they are paid for never get paid for more than they do.

An ounce of loyalty is worth a pound of cleverness.

Give me a man, who instead of always telling you what should be done, goes ahead and does it. Initiative is doing the right thing without being told.

There is no failure except in no longer trying. There is no defeat except from within, no insurmountable barrier except our own inherent weakness of purpose.

If pleasures are greatest in anticipation, just remember that this is also true of trouble.

If you have no enemies you are apt to be in the same predicament in regard to friends.

The greatest mistake a man can make is to be afraid of making one.

The highest reward that God gives us for good work is the ability to do better work.

LILLIAN GILBRETH

American management consultant and reformer, 1878–1972

Lillian and Frank Gilbreth were dedicated revolutionaries who changed forever the way that American capital dealt with their workers and, in the process, changed our concept of time as an integral element in production.

In spite of her father's objections to educated women, Lillian Moller attended the University of California at Berkeley. She graduated with a degree in literature in 1900, received her MA two years later and by 1915 had earned a doctoral degree in psychology from Brown.

Between degrees, she met and married Frank Gilbreth, a former bricklayer who was fascinated with time and motion studies as a tool for improving worker output. Together they pioneered the use of moving pictures and sequential still photography to investigate the movements necessary to perform repetitive jobs.

While Frank concentrated on the technical aspects of worker efficiency, Lillian was attracted to the human side of the equation, being among the first people to recognize the effects of physical and mental stress on workers. Together they wrote 12 books on management techniques; they also produced an equal number of children.

Running their ever-expanding household with the efficiency they advocated in their books, Frank and Lillian Gilbreth's popular claim to fame came in a book written by two of their children, *Cheaper by the Dozen*. The exploits of Frank, Lillian and their brood was brought to the screen in 1950.

Frank had died in 1924, leaving Lillian to carry on the work alone. Between Frank's death, and her own nearly half a century later, Lillian Gilbreth continued to study and campaign for efficient use of human resources. She produced more than 14 books, kept up an endless round of lecture tours and still fulfilled the duties of a professor of management at Purdue University. Lillian Gilbreth may well have qualified as the world's first 'super Mom'.

The selections below are all taken from the book *The Foreman in Manpower Management* by Lillian Gilbreth and Alice Rice Cook (reproduced with kind permission of The McGraw-Hill Companies). Written in 1947 the book is directed to post-war industrial production, so such terms at 'foreman' and 'supervisor' are in constant use. The message, however, is as relevant today as it was half a century ago. The passages have been rearranged by category, under our headings, for the sake of consistency.

DEALING WITH SUPERIORS

Top management expects the foreman to be a morale builder. One of the greatest morale factors is loyalty to a common goal. Mutual interest and identification among employees build and strengthen loyalty. When both foreman and worker feel they are engaged in something larger than their own job, their satisfaction grows. Mere loyalty to a person can never take the place of loyalty to a common goal.

> When the boss is excited about something, it is your job to make the workers excited about it too, no matter what your personal thoughts are. If you seriously disagree with the boss, discuss it with them in private, never let the workers know you think it is a stupid idea.

Criticisms or suggestions by your employer as to ways in which your department might run more effectively can have one of three effects on you. 1) You can fight back, attempt to alibi, blame your associates and show a resentful attitude. 2) You can be crushed and humiliated, and feel that probably this is the beginning of the end. 3) You can accept the criticism objectively and discuss ways in which the situation might be improved.

Even in what seems to be unfair blame there is usually at least one grain of truth. Realize that suggesting change may indicate your supervisor's real interest in the department and you.

When called in for a discussion of general policy; the foreman has a fine opportunity to submit his own constructive ideas.

> In the same way you may change things among your workers, the boss may make changes in middle management that you may not agree with. Don't take it personally but, at the same time, don't simply accept something that you think will decrease the effectiveness of your people. Stand up for yourself and your people. Just remember, in the end the boss has the final say. If you lose, let it go and don't brood about it.

THE ROLE OF MIDDLE MANAGEMENT

The foreman has been delegated the most important type of supervision in industrial production. The worker looks to him for direction, supervision and help. Top management, through its techniques of delegating, puts much power in his hands, including that of manpower control. Industry sets up a variety of services to help him do his job. It is his job not only to use the resources he has in handling the manpower under his supervision, but also to find out what is available and get hold of that material.

> Middle management is obviously a position of great responsibility. They are the bridge between top management and the workforce and it is their job to make use of every resource at their disposal to carry out their job effectively.

The foreman is expected to carry out and interpret company policies. This responsibility demands the use of clear, forceful language, the art of persuasion and a knowledge of the facts involved. He alone is responsible for seeing that the worker knows what the company wants. Only through the closest co-operation with top management can the foreman be in possession of all the facts. Only through the closest co-operation with the worker can the foreman know how these policies should be explained so that they can be understood and followed with satisfaction.

> Middle management must act as a two-way conduit between top management and the workforce. This means that they must be able to speak fluently with those above them and those below them.

The foreman must recognize that over 50% of his job is a human relations job. The foreman is born into human relations and remains a part of them throughout his life. If he gets on well with himself and his family, he has the fundamentals on which to build other successful human relations.

Certainly a person who cannot connect with people outside the workplace will never be able to do so on the job.

The ability to inspire others with confidence in themselves and in the company is a must for good personnel relations. To accomplish this goal the foreman practises what good foremen have always practised. He keeps his promises, always, even under the most difficult circumstances. He stands up for his men and women, even in the face of criticism. He examines all evidence before making a decision. He makes certain that fairness exists in respect to such items as overtime, discipline, transfer, promotions and assignment of work. He has definite reasons for the things he does and is ready to explain them to those who have a right to such explanations. The loyalty and confidence of employees treated in such a way become a shock absorber in time of stress and strain and often prevent the breaking up of a formerly smooth-running department.

High personal standards, determination and the ability to inspire others with enthusiasm are essential qualities in an effective middle manager.

When the foreman has the ability to see himself in relationship to the entire organization, as well as the part he plays in his own department, his planning achieves an overall value to the whole organization. He then not only plans for the work that his own employees do but also helps them see how their job fits into the entire production of the plant. When he and his employees develop an awareness of the policies and problems of supervision and management, production becomes of individual concern to each employee.

It is essential to keep in mind the 'big picture' and pass it on to those under your control. Only then can the general workforce understand that their jobs are essential to the smooth running of the company as a whole.

Not only must the supervisor recognize his relations with the employee as a person, but also the employee must recognize his responsibility towards other employees. This applies to every relationship in industry. The judgement of the supervisor, for example, is influenced by his relationship with his superior and with other employees. If he has established sound human relationships in every part of the operating department, his judgement is free to cope with problems of personnel and production in an effective way.

> Like the item above, only when middle managers understand their own importance in the greater scheme of things can they feel comfortable passing information back and forth between top management and the workforce.

In carrying out the responsibilities of leadership, the foreman emphasizes equally all three functions of his job – personnel, production and industrialization. Whether he is dealing with a problem employee, a delay in the production schedule or a change of method, the same avenues of communication must be used to build co-operation and confidence in everyone concerned. Since learning comes more through discussion and agreement than through controversy, good listening habits are a must for a foreman. He loses no opportunity to demonstrate his competence; this leads to strengthening his function as a liaison person between his department and top management.

> Don't get bogged down in a single aspect of your job. Be alert to subtle changes in those around you so that you can keep every aspect of your department running smoothly.

The wise foreman knows he can do much to change top management's concept of leadership. Through his handling of problems he can prove that supervision is more than merely carrying messages or policing the workers.

As we are about to see, middle management cannot function properly if it is simply a messenger for the top brass. They must make the bosses understand the needs of the workers, of which they may not always be aware.

The morale of a foreman who is treated like a messenger is depressing. Being treated like a messenger boy not only has a bad effect on the foreman himself but may also lead to unhappy employee relations; the worker cannot look with respect to a foreman who has no authority.

If you, as a middle manager, do not command the respect of your superiors, you cannot expect it from those in your charge. Sometimes it is more difficult to convince top management of your worth than it is to convince those beneath you. Make this a top priority.

The successful foreman must be able to decide on the appropriate things for him to do and delegate what can be delegated satisfactorily. As long as he retains the experimental point of view towards planning, then the plan will remain his servant. But beware of the time when the plan assumes power in its own right, for there is no harder taskmaster than a 'must' plan.

Don't become rigid in your thinking or slave to a set of plans. Remain flexible and allow any plans to change as they are brought towards implementation.

The really good planner has a flexibility that enables him to face reversal and success with equanimity and a sense of humour. A plan, he knows, can be only the first step and must never supersede the human values, which may slow up production much more than a momentary change in his plan.

The success of a plan is never assured until it is tried. If it fails, don't get discouraged and always keep in mind that any plan only works if it works at all levels, from top management through to the rank and file.

If the foreman has to delegate any of his responsibilities it should be in the operational end of his job; human relations being kept as his first responsibility.

It is easier, and often more effective, if purely mechanical tasks are delegated rather than allowing the role of personnel co-ordinator to slip from your hands.

Sooner or later, like all people, foremen are faced with the necessity of evaluating their job abilities. Either they can wait until life forces them to evaluate themselves or they can do it before they are forced to. The realization by the foreman that he is constantly being measured by top management, his associates and his subordinates is a spur to self-evaluation.

In the same way that you must keep ahead of problems around you, you must also keep ahead of your own. It is always easier to solve other people's problems than your own, but if you are not functioning properly, you cannot deal with others effectively.

The foreman should ask himself the question: 'Am I growing in my ability to lead?' There is nothing static in the business of leadership. The leader is always in the process of becoming more effective or less effective in handling relationships and situations.

Stagnation in the workplace is absolutely fatal, particularly if you expect advancement.

DEALING WITH THE WORKFORCE

The foreman finds the establishment of satisfactory human relations his most important job. He must sense any early signs of manpower trouble and do all that he can to prevent it, both within and beyond his own department. If he sees that faulty human relations are developing anywhere in the organization, he will try to get word to the right person to handle the problem.

> Here again, it is a matter of being able to see the 'big picture'. Those who can even spot potential problems outside their assigned area, will quickly make themselves invaluable to top management.

In addition to the need for economic and job security, every employee desires 1) to be accepted by a group; 2) to have friends; 3) to receive recognition and appreciation; 4) to feel necessary and see his place in the organization; 5) to have an opportunity to talk things over; 6) to make the most of himself.

> This is what everyone, from the top down, wants, and while they may not get everything they want, it is your job, as a middle manager, to do your best to keep them moving in the right direction.

When a person feels appreciated, he feels necessary. When he feels necessary, he sees his place in the entire organization. From the first day in the department the worker should be able to see himself in relationship to the department and the entire organization, not only as a worker but as a person.

> Don't allow your workers to feel isolated from the general goings on. Keep them aware of what's happening elsewhere and make them see that their job is just as important as anyone elses.

Only a well-adjusted worker in the right job justifies the large investment of time and money made by the company in hiring, training and maintaining him.

> As a middle manager, it is your job to keep people working to the best of their ability. If you spot someone of real ability in a 'no brainer' job, you should try to make better use of their talent. They will thank you and so will top management.

It is wise for the foreman to be constantly looking for employees who deserve, or could qualify for, promotion, and to watch both their operating and their personnel techniques. The product of such awareness is a group of workers who appreciate that their foreman has their advancement in mind.

> Everyone wants to be recognized. If your people know you have your eye on them in a positive way, they will be more likely to do their best work.

An employee's promotion should be put through as soon as the decision has been made. . . so as to utilize the upflare of ambition which has taken place in the employee and add to the pleasure which the whole experience is supposed to give him.

> Nothing is more demoralizing than being promised a promotion and then waiting months for it to go through. If this happens, the enthusiasm that made the person worthy of advancement may wither and be lost forever.

If other employees have been passed over when a person is promoted, the reasons for this should be explained to them in detail. Otherwise the promoted employee may find himself in an impossible situation as far as relationships with his co-workers are concerned.

Charges of favouritism or antagonism make up some of the most annoying problems of the foreman. The foreman must remember that everything he does, says or feels will have reverberations not only through the department but also throughout the organization.

> This is the problem that makes it almost impossible to form a real friendship with one of the many people who work for you. It is a sad truth, but a truth none the less.

The foreman is in a strategic position to eliminate causes of friction between his workers. He will want to make certain that he himself is not guilty of bearing employees grudges or harbouring resentment in any situation and is doing everything possible to smooth out such feelings in the department.

> This can be very difficult, but you must remain impartial to all of the employees. Remember, your position already sets you apart from them: do nothing that will make that gap more apparent than it already is.

When the employee understands the foreman's relationship to the entire organization, he has taken the first step toward understanding not only his own function but also that of capital, administration and planning. When the worker sees that the foreman is expected to call on specialists for the help he may need, he sees why he, himself, is expected to call on the foreman when he needs help.

> Make certain your people know that you, like them, are just one link in a very long chain. When you need help you seek it out and they should always feel free to do the same thing: in this case, it probably means that they will come to you. If they are afraid to approach you, that cannot happen and efficiency will break down.

The foreman who gives his employees credit for at least average intelligence will find that they can offer an amazing number of helpful suggestions. The foreman who fears making use of good suggestions is certainly not developing leaders among his men. The minute the atmosphere of a department is filled with criticism, employees begin questioning each other's motives and build walls to avoid criticism.

> Talk 'with' your people not 'at' them. Let them know that you are interested in what they think. Listen to them and take their ideas under serious consideration.

How orders are given can far outweigh the order itself. The cowboy's slogan, 'Smile when you say that, partner' can well be a motto for such procedures.

No matter how frustrated you are, never let it get in the way of keeping friendly relations with your people.

EFFECTIVE USE OF MANPOWER

Progressive management knows that manpower control underlies and determines all other cost controls. The justification of each employee's place on the payroll is a major responsibility in establishing manpower control.

What do we mean by manpower control? To put it simply, manpower control is the planning, setting up and maintenance of conditions under which a man can function at top efficiency. This includes not only economic and physical conditions but also the psychological. This requires the full utilization of each employee's ability at the highest level of his potential – the right man for the right job and the right job for the man.

Both of the above items tell us to make the best use of your people. Never hire more people than you need and see to it that the ones you have are being used to best advantage. It is a tall order, but essential if you are going to avoid waste.

The foreman should know the kind and amount of skill needed for every job in his department and the kind and amount of training needed to produce this skill.

The middle manager needs to know almost as much about every job under their control as the people doing the job.

Among the questions the foreman may ask himself are:
1) Could the employee contribute more to production on another job than on this one?

2) Is he temperamentally and emotionally ready for promotion?

It is just as unfair to demand more of someone than they can produce as it is to under-utilize their talents.

There must be flexibility in functions and relationships if manpower control is to be effective. Just as the individual is free to act intelligently when he has himself under complete control, so a group is free to achieve the best results only when its members are under control.

If your people are only doing half a job, the department is not in control: rearrange things until it functions properly.

BIBLIOGRAPHY/PERMISSION
ACKNOWLEDGEMENTS

Every effort has been made to trace all copyright holders, but if any have been overlooked, the authors and the publishers will be pleased to make necessary amendments at the first opportunity.

Benjamin Franklin: *The Life Essays of Dr Franklin*, T Kinnersley, London (1816)

Confucius: *The Analects* adapted from 'Zongwen' the Chinese National Cultural website for Middle Kingdom Literature

Edward I: *The Statutes at Large*, Vol I, Mark Basket, London (1763)

Elbert Hubbard: Adapted from the Roycrofters website

Elizabeth I: *The Virgin Queen*, Christopher Hibbert, Guild Publishing, London (1990)
The Life and Times of Elizabeth I, Neville Williams, Weidenfeld and Nicolson, London (1972)
Elizabeth the Great, Elizabeth Jenkins, Coward-McCann Inc, New York, (1959)
The Statutes at Large, Vol II, Mark Basket, London (1763)

Frank B Gilbreth Jr and Ernestine Gilbreth, *Cheaper by the Dozen*, Bantam Doubleday, 1981

Hammurabi: Hammurabi's Code adapted from the Avalon Project at the Yale Law School. Translated by LW King

Helena Rubinstein: *Madame: An Intimate Biography of Helena Rubinstein*, Patrick O'Higgins, Weidenfeld and Nicolson, London (1971)

Hildegard von Bingen: *The Letters of Hildegard of Bingen,* Vols I and II, Joseph L Baird and Radd K Ehrman, Oxford University Press, New York, 1994 & 1998

HJ Heinz: *The Good Provider, HJ Heinz and his 57 Varieties*, Robert C Alberts. Copyright © 1973 by Robert C Alberts. Reprinted by permission of Houghton Mifflin Company. All rights reserved

King John: Magna Carta adapted from the Avalon project website at Yale Law School

Lillian Gilbreth: *The Foreman in Manpower Management*, L Gilbreth and Alice Rice Cook, McGraw-Hill Book Company, Inc, New York, 1947

Lillian Vernon: *An Eye for Winners*, Lillian Vernon, HarperCollins, New York (1996)

Machiavelli: *The Prince and Other Pieces*, Routledge (1883)

Moses: Laws of Moses and The Ten Commandments/*The Holy Bible*, King James version, World Syndicate Publishing, Cleveland, Ohio (1939)

Pirate Code: *A General History of the Most Notorious Pyrates*, Captain Charles Johnson (probably a pseudonym for Daniel Defoe), Ch. Rivington, London (1724)

Pope Gregory I: *Bede's Ecclesiastical History of England*, Henry G Bohn, London (1847)

Solomon: *The Holy Bible*, King James version, World Syndicate Publishing, Cleveland, Ohio (1939)

Sun Tzu: *The Art of War*, PF Collier, London (1910) as found on Project Gutenburg Etext

William Shakespeare: Adapted from *Hamlet, Prince of Denmark* and *The Merchant of Venice* as found in, *Shakespeare: the Complete Works*, Clark & Wright